D0734871

SHEILAH'S EASY WAYS TO ELEGANT COOKING

SHEILAH'S EASY WAYS TO ELEGANT COOKING

The Fearless Fussless Cookbook by

Sheilah Kaufman

DELACORTE PRESS/ELEANOR FRIEDE

Published by
Delacorte Press/Eleanor Friede
1 Dag Hammarskjold Plaza
New York, N.Y. 10017

Manufactured in the United States of America

Second Printing—1980

Designed by Giorgetta Bell McRee

LIBRARY OF CONGRESS CATALOGING IN PUBLICATION DATA

Kaufman, Sheilah.
Sheilah's easy ways to elegant cooking.

Includes index.
1. Cookery.   I. Title.
II. Title: Easy ways to elegant cooking.
TX715.K2025   641.5   78-26188

ISBN 0-440-07959-4

Acknowledgment

Many thanks to all my family members and friends for gamely testing the recipes contained herein, for contributing a few of their own favorites, and for encouraging me to share them in a cookbook. And a special thanks to my long-time collaborator, Cinnie Manuel, who helped interpret my nonchalant approach to cooking with wisdom and clarity so that this book could be written.

Contents

SHEILAH'S EASY WAYS TO ELEGANT COOKING

Introduction

Despite all the evidence that America has discovered fine cooking, I have found that many people still don't like to cook because they are afraid. Either they are intimidated by intricate recipes and by doctrinaire cooking authorities, or they lack the confidence to experiment with new dishes.

But it's all in the way you think about it. Think of cooking as fun and carefree, and it will be!

I love to eat and to entertain, but I don't like to spend endless hours in the kitchen. As a result, I have evolved my own culinary philosophy that takes the fear and fuss out of cooking.

I am not a perfectionist when it comes to cooking. I believe it is very hard to ruin most "gourmet" dishes. I will not, for example, allow myself to be driven to tears by a pastry recipe that tells me to roll the dough to $\frac{1}{16}$-inch thickness. I'll roll the dough only until I think I cannot get it any thinner, or until it cracks—whichever comes first. I always end up patching anyway, but the results seem to be satisfactory, and that is what counts.

Perhaps my crêpes aren't perfectly shaped circles, or maybe they have holes. But, after they are filled, rolled, and covered with a good-tasting sauce, who is going to be any the wiser?

Don't misunderstand me; if you can execute recipes flawlessly, so much the better. But if not, do the best you can. Nor am I suggesting that you be slipshod. You should always read and follow recipes carefully. I feel, however, that with modern life-styles it's unrealistic to expect most people to slave for hours in the interests of culinary perfection.

As long as your dishes look appealing and taste good, few people will notice your sins of omission or commission.

Your guests will be so appreciative of your hospitality that they will enjoy your efforts, even if the results are slightly flawed. So why worry about it? The company is the point of the get-together; the food is merely a catalyst. Unless you, as a cook, can enjoy yourself, what fun is there in entertaining?

I have developed a style of cooking for company that enables me to prepare everything in advance, with just a few small tasks or a final reheating left until the last minute. That's why, before my guests arrive, I will be found reading a book.

That may sound improbable, but I believe that you cannot be a good host or hostess if you are not relaxed. You should not be in the kitchen fretting over a temperamental Hollandaise sauce while your guests are cooling their heels in the living room. By selecting recipes that entail a maximum of advance preparation and a minimum of last-minute attention, you can feel like a guest at your own party!

And that's what you'll find in this book: a varied assortment of tempting recipes designed for easy entertaining and family dining as well. Such flavorful dishes as Shrimp Mousse, Beef Bourguignon, Chicken Cordon Bleu, Manicotti, Hawaiian Sweet Potatoes, Chocolate Marble Cheesecake, and Strawberry Bavarian will be the hit of any party, and they can be prepared at your convenience and refrigerated or frozen until needed. In the few instances when advance preparation is not feasible (such as most Oriental dishes or a baked soufflé), I tell you how to do as much as possible beforehand so that you can still serve these delectable dishes to company without tearing your hair out.

Throughout the book I have sprinkled liberally many useful "Hints" which will make your cooking life easier. I learned them the hard way, and they seem so simple you won't believe how much they will help you.

Most of the recipes in this book will serve from 6 to 8 people —which I believe is an ideal size for a friendly, intimate dinner party. There are, additionally, several recipes that are better suited to large gatherings. In virtually every case, you can easily double the recipe to meet your particular entertaining needs. With the exception of most baked goods, you can also cut many of my recipes in half if you like; but I think it makes more sense to prepare the entire recipe and to freeze half for future use.

All of these recipes have passed the ultimate test: They have been tried and approved by family, friends, and students across the country.

I hope that they will become your favorites, too, and that this book will help you think of cooking as the enjoyable experience it's meant to be.

—Sheilah Kaufman

Basic Equipment Checklist

Do not be scared off by the length of this list; chances are you already have most of the items in your kitchen. Those utensils that you do not have will be a worthwhile investment because they can all be used repeatedly in many different recipes.

COOKING UTENSILS, GADGETS, AND APPLIANCES

Two or three wooden or melamine spoons (Superior to metal because they don't get hot, and they won't scratch your pans.)
Large "balloon" wire whisk (for beating eggs)
Small wire whisk (for mixing sauces and gravies)
Rubber scraper
Potato masher
2-pronged cooking fork
Tongs
Spatula
Slotted spoon
4-inch paring knife
10-inch carbon-steel chef's knife (Carbon steel holds a cutting edge better than stainless, and it is now available with a rustproof coating.)

Sharpening steel (to keep your chef's knife razor-sharp)

Vegetable peeler

Garlic press

"Mouli" grater (for cheese, citrus peel, nuts, chocolate)

3-inch round cookie cutter

Rolling pin and stockingette (cover for rolling pin to prevent sticking)

Sieve or strainer

Colander

Wire cake racks

Acrylic cutting board (Preferable to wood because it does not absorb odors or bacteria, and it can be easily washed.)

Pastry blender (for cutting shortening into flour)

Sifter

4-cup liquid measuring cup (with pouring lip)

Set of individual dry measuring cups ($\frac{1}{4}$-, $\frac{1}{3}$-, $\frac{1}{2}$-, $\frac{2}{3}$-, $\frac{3}{4}$- and 1-cup size; use these to measure dry ingredients by filling them and leveling off the top with a knife)

Two sets of measuring spoons (one for liquid, one for dry ingredients)

Electric mixer (You will find the stationary kind infinitely easier to work with, especially when something must be beaten for several minutes.)

1-, 2- and 3-quart mixing bowls (in addition to the ones that come with your electric mixer)

Blender

Food processor (I hesitate to list this as a "necessity" because even the moderately priced ones are expensive. If, however, you invest in one, you will not need as many knives, graters, or other gadgets. It can also eliminate the need for a blender. It is not, however, recommended for whipping cream or egg whites. But the food processor simplifies many tedious cooking chores, and for the busy cook it is a blessing.)

COOKING/BAKING VESSELS

Large shallow baking dish (for chicken, paella, lasagne, etc.)
4-quart casserole with cover
2-quart casserole with cover
2½-quart straight-sided soufflé dish
Two or three 9-inch round cake pans
9-inch glass pie pan
9 × 13 × 2-inch baking pan (for sheet cakes, bar cookies, certain main dishes, and vegetable casseroles)
9 × 9 × 2-inch baking pan
One or two 9 × 5 × 3-inch loaf pans (for yeast and quick breads)
10-inch tube pan (with removable bottom) or "Bundt" pan
9-inch springform pan
1- and 3-quart saucepans (Preferably copper or enamel-coated cast iron, as these are the best conductors of heat, and they won't react with high-acid substances, such as vinegar and wine.)
7- or 8-inch steel crêpe pan
14-inch steel wok
5-quart kettle or Dutch oven
12-inch skillet
One or two 18-inch cookie sheets
One or two muffin pans
Double boiler
4- and 6-cup molds

Chapter 1
APPETIZERS

Meat

Fish & Seafood

Cheese

Vegetables

Dips

Soups

The American style of entertaining is such that most cooks serve appetizers—or hors d'oeuvres—with drinks before seating their guests at the dinner table. I follow this custom mainly because it allows time for the main dishes that I have prepared in advance to reheat. Drinks and appetizers before dinner also help to put everyone at ease, and latecomers can arrive during this "social hour" without disrupting the dinner.

When selecting hors d'oeuvres, keep your dinner menu in mind. A rich dinner calls for simple hors d'oeuvres, such as marinated vegetables. Those made with cheese or sour cream are a pleasant prelude to an uncomplicated main dish, such as steak or pot roast. Appetizers made with meat or seafood are best suited to cocktail buffets; they can also be served before simple, meatless dinners.

Call them appetizers or hors d'oeuvres, but make them part of your next get-together. Most of the recipes in this chapter are for "finger foods," but for more formal occasions, I've provided a few items that should be served at the table, including some of my favorite soup recipes.

Meat

COUNTRY PÂTÉ EN CASSEROLE

A simplified version of the classic French pâté, this will be the pièce de résistance *at any gathering. For an authentic touch, serve with slices of crusty French bread (never crackers), sweet butter, and gherkins.*

---

  1 pound calf liver
  ¾ pound ground pork fat
  ¼ pound ground veal
  3 tablespoons butter
  1 large onion, finely chopped
  5 tablespoons flour
  1⅓ cups milk
  3 eggs
  2 tablespoons brandy
  2 teaspoons salt
  ½ teaspoon freshly ground pepper
     Pinch of allspice
     Pinch of mace
  6 slices bacon
  ¼ pound small whole mushrooms, wiped clean

Rinse the liver, and dry with paper towels. Purée the liver in a food processor, or put it in a blender container—one-third at a time—and blend at high speed until smooth.

Place the puréed liver in a bowl, and combine it with the pork fat and ground veal.

Melt the butter in a small saucepan over medium heat, and sauté the onion until tender, but not browned—about 5 minutes.

Stir in the flour until well combined.

Gradually add the milk, stirring constantly, and bring to boiling. Reduce heat, and simmer 1 minute.

Add the sauce to the meat mixture, along with the eggs, brandy, and seasonings, stirring until well blended.

Grease an attractive 2-quart casserole, and turn the liver mixture into the casserole.

Place the casserole in a roasting pan or large baking pan, and pour hot water about 2 inches deep around the casserole.

Bake, uncovered, at 350 degrees for 1¾ hours.

Let the pâté cool at least one hour before serving. If not serving right away, refrigerate it until needed.

About 15 minutes before serving, sauté the bacon in a large skillet until crisp. Drain on paper towels, leaving the pieces intact.

Pour off all but 2 tablespoons of the drippings. In the remaining bacon drippings, sauté the mushrooms until golden over medium heat.

Arrange the mushrooms and bacon slices over the pâté in decorative fashion, and serve with bread, sweet butter, and gherkins.

Serves 18 to 20.

SAUERKRAUT BALLS

You won't believe how good sauerkraut can taste until you try this recipe.

---

1 can (16 ounces) sauerkraut, well drained
1 pound ground beef
1 medium onion, finely chopped
2 tablespoons flour
2 eggs
¾ to 1 cup mashed potatoes
2 cups cracker crumbs
   Oil for deep-frying

Using a kitchen shears, snip the sauerkraut into small pieces.

In a medium bowl, combine the sauerkraut with the ground beef and onion, mixing well.

Stir in the flour, eggs, and mashed potatoes until well blended.

Form the mixture into 1-inch balls, and roll the balls in the cracker crumbs, coating well.

Fill a deep-fat fryer or a deep skillet with about 2 inches of oil; heat to 400 degrees. Use a deep-fat thermometer if your utensil is not equipped with one.

Fry the balls in hot oil until golden-brown on all sides. Drain well on paper towels.

Serve hot. If not serving right away, wrap the balls in foil and freeze until needed. To reheat, place directly from freezer into a 400-degree oven, wrapped in foil.

Makes about 6 dozen balls.

SATAY

An exotic dish that is sure to win raves.

SAUCE:

  1 large onion, grated
  2 garlic cloves, minced
  1 tablespoon chili powder
  1 tablespoon vegetable oil
  2 teaspoons ground coriander
  1 teaspoon ground cumin
  6 tablespoons chunky peanut butter
1½ cups coconut milk (not juice)
  3 tablespoons packed brown sugar
  2 tablespoons soy sauce
  2 tablespoons lemon juice

  1 pound round steak, cut into ½-inch strips
  1 pound chicken livers, halved
  2 chicken breasts, skinned, boned, and cut into small pieces
¼ cup soy sauce (approx.)
¼ cup dry cocktail sherry (approx.)

In a large saucepan, combine the grated onion with the minced garlic, chili powder, and oil. Cook over medium heat for 2 minutes.

Add the coriander and cumin; cook another 5 minutes.

Add the remaining sauce ingredients, stirring well. Simmer until thickened; set aside.

About 30 minutes before serving, preheat the oven to broil.

Thread the steak, liver, and chicken alternately on 8 to 12 bamboo skewers. Lay the skewers on a cake rack over a shallow ovenproof baking dish.

Sprinkle the meat with equal parts of the soy sauce and sherry, coating each piece.

Broil the meat, 6 inches from heat, for 3 to 5 minutes, turning once.

While the meat is broiling, gently reheat the sauce. Transfer the sauce to an attractive serving bowl, and let your guests dip skewers of meat in the sauce.

Serves 8 to 12.

Note: The Satay Sauce, at room temperature, also can be used as an unusual dressing for any vegetable salad.

RUMAKI

Even people who dislike liver will enjoy this recipe.

---

12 chicken livers, halved
½ cup soy sauce
12 water chestnuts (canned), cut in half
12 slices bacon, halved
 1 cup dark brown sugar, packed

Several hours before serving, put the chicken liver halves in a small shallow bowl, and pour the soy sauce in. Refrigerate, covered, at least 4 hours.

About 40 minutes before serving, drain the soy sauce from the chicken livers, and reserve.

Place a water chestnut half next to each piece of liver, and wrap half a slice of bacon around the two; secure with a toothpick.

Dip each rumaki in the brown sugar, coating well.

Place the rumaki on a cake rack in a shallow ovenproof dish or pan. Pour the reserved soy sauce over the rumaki.

Bake at 375 degrees for 20 to 30 minutes, turning occasionally to brown evenly, until the bacon is crisp.

Drain the rumaki on paper towels for 1 minute; serve hot.

Makes 2 dozen.

BACON WRAPS

Unusual, easy, and flavorful.

---

1 box (1 pound) Waverly soda crackers
1 pound bacon

Separate the crackers in half along the perforations.

Cut each bacon slice in half.

Wrap one-half strip of bacon around each cracker, pressing the ends together firmly.

Place the bacon wraps on a rack set in a shallow baking pan.

Bake the wraps at 350 degrees for 20 to 25 minutes, or until the bacon is cooked.

Quickly drain the bacon wraps on paper towels, and serve hot.

Makes about 3 dozen.

ZESTY MEATBALLS

1 pound ground beef
Salt and freshly ground pepper to taste
½ teaspoon garlic powder
1 small onion, grated
1 egg
1 jar (12 ounces) chili sauce
1½ cups water
6 gingersnap cookies, crumbled
⅓ cup brown sugar, packed
1 cup raisins

In a large bowl, combine the meat, salt, pepper, garlic powder, grated onion and the egg, mixing well.

Shape into small meatballs, about 1 inch in diameter.

Pour the chili sauce into a medium saucepan. Fill the empty chili sauce jar with the water, and stir into the chili sauce.

Add the crumbled gingersnaps, sugar, and raisins to the chili sauce, stirring to mix well.

Place the meatballs in the sauce, and cook, covered, over medium-low heat for 25 to 30 minutes. For a thicker sauce, remove the pot lid during the last 10 minutes of cooking.

Serve the meatballs in a chafing dish with toothpicks.

The meatballs may be frozen and reheated in the top part of a double boiler over boiling water.

Makes 2½ to 3 dozen.

HINT

To keep brown sugar from hardening, store it in a container with a tight-fitting lid along with a piece of bread.

Fish and Seafood

CHINESE PEPPER SHRIMP

A wok (Oriental-style frying pan) is a must to prepare this spicy hors d'oeuvre.

---

2 scallions, finely minced (including the green tops)
2 teaspoons powdered ginger
1 tablespoon catsup
1 tablespoon chili sauce
1 tablespoon dry cocktail sherry
1 tablespoon soy sauce
1 teaspoon sugar
2 tablespoons peanut oil
1 pound shrimp, shelled and deveined
   Pinch of salt
¼ to ½ teaspoon dried crushed red pepper (depending on how hot you'd like the shrimp to be)

In a small bowl, mix together the scallions, ginger, catsup, chili sauce, sherry, soy sauce, and sugar; set aside.

Heat the oil in a wok over medium heat for 2 minutes. Add the shrimp, and cook, stirring, just until the color begins to change. Stir in the scallion mixture, blending well.

Add the salt and red pepper, and continue stirring until the shrimp are done. Do not overcook the shrimp; about 3 minutes will do.

To serve, spear with toothpicks.

Serves 6.

Note: For a main course, you can double this recipe and serve the shrimp over boiled white rice. The doubled recipe will serve 4.

SHRIMP IN MUSTARD SAUCE

SHRIMP:

  3 quarts water
  1 tablespoon pickling spice
2½ pounds shrimp

SAUCE:

⅓ cup chopped parsley
¼ cup finely chopped shallots
¼ cup tarragon vinegar
¼ cup red wine vinegar
½ cup olive oil
 4 tablespoons Dijon mustard
 2 teaspoons dried crushed red pepper
   Salt and freshly ground pepper to taste

Place the water in a large kettle with the pickling spice. (These will give off a fragrant aroma as the shrimp cook.)

Bring the water to a boil, and add the shrimp. Cook only for 3 to 4 minutes—until the shrimp turn pink. Do not overcook.

Drain the shrimp, and when they are cool enough to handle, shell and devein them.

Transfer the shrimp to a large refrigerator dish.

To make the sauce, combine all the sauce ingredients in a small bowl, mixing well.

Pour the sauce over the shrimp, turning to coat the shrimp well.

Cover, and refrigerate for several hours or overnight.

Serve cold, speared with toothpicks.

Serves 10 to 12.

SHRIMP BALLS

An Oriental-style appetizer that is guaranteed to disappear quickly.

2½ pounds shrimp, shelled and deveined
 3 cans (6¾ ounces each) water chestnuts, well drained
 3 egg whites, lightly beaten
 1 bunch scallions, thinly sliced (including green tops)
1½ tablespoons salt
1½ tablespoons soy sauce
 1 tablespoon dry cocktail sherry
 ½ tablespoon MSG (optional)
 1 tablespoon cornstarch
    Oil for deep-frying

Finely chop the shrimp, using a food processor; or chop them, a handful at a time, with a chef's knife.

Finely chop the water chestnuts and place them in a bowl with the shrimp.

Add the egg whites, sliced scallions, salt, soy sauce, sherry, optional MSG, and the cornstarch, mixing well.

Taste for seasoning and add more salt if desired.

Shape the mixture into balls the size of walnuts.

In a large skillet or deep-fat fryer heat about 2 inches of oil to 375 degrees. If your fryer is not equipped with a thermometer, use a deep-fat thermometer.

Fry the balls until golden on all sides; drain on paper towels and serve hot with mustard and/or sweet and sour sauce.

Shrimp balls can also be frozen at this point. Reheat them on an ungreased cookie sheet at 350 degrees for 10 to 15 minutes, or until heated through.

Makes about 3½ dozen.

SHRIMP MOUSSE

A popular molded appetizer that is perfect for feeding a crowd.

1½ tablespoons unflavored gelatin
 ¼ cup cold water
 1 can (10¾ ounces) condensed tomato soup, undiluted
 3 packages (3 ounces each) cream cheese, softened
 1 cup mayonnaise
 ¾ cup finely chopped celery
1½ cups finely chopped cooked shrimp (Frozen cooked shrimp
      can be used; defrost according to package directions.)
 1 medium onion, finely chopped

Several hours or the day before serving, soak the gelatin in the cold water to soften.

In a small saucepan, over medium heat, bring the tomato soup to a boil.

Add the gelatin mixture, stirring well to dissolve it. Remove the saucepan from the heat, and let cool.

When the soup mixture has cooled, add the softened cream cheese and mayonnaise, blending well.

Mix in the celery, shrimp, and onion.

Pour the mixture into a lightly oiled 6-cup mold, and refrigerate several hours or overnight.

Unmold onto a large serving platter (see Hint, page 23), and serve with unflavored crackers or miniature rye bread.

Serves 12 to 16.

HINT

To make your own wine vinegar from leftover wines that have begun to turn sour, add 2 tablespoons of red wine vinegar to 1 cup of red wine, or 2 tablespoons of white wine vinegar to 1 cup of white wine. Let stand, uncovered, at room temperature for 36 hours. Store in a jar with a tight-fitting lid.

CRAB MOUSSE

2 envelopes unflavored gelatin
2 tablespoons dry cocktail sherry
1 cup chicken broth
2 egg yolks
1 cup heavy cream
3 tablespoons lemon juice
2 cups crab meat, flaked, with all shell and cartilage removed
5 drops Tabasco sauce
2 tablespoons finely chopped scallion (including some of the green tops)
2 stalks celery, finely chopped
1½ tablespoons chopped parsley
Pinch of dried marjoram
Pinch of dried thyme
½ cup mayonnaise

Two or three days before serving, place the gelatin and sherry in a blender container, and blend at low speed for 1 minute.

Bring the chicken broth to a boil in a small saucepan, then remove from the heat and add to the gelatin; blend at low speed for 10 seconds.

Add the egg yolks, cream, lemon juice, crab meat, Tabasco sauce, scallion, celery, parsley, and herbs to the blender container.

Blend at low speed for 10 seconds, or until the mixture is smooth.

If your blender container is large enough, add the mayonnaise, and blend for another 10 seconds. If it is not large enough, pour the mixture into a large bowl and, with a wire whisk, beat in the mayonnaise.

Pour the mixture into a lightly oiled 6-cup mold. Cover with aluminum foil, and refrigerate for at least 2 days.

Just before serving, unmold the mousse onto a large serving platter, using directions in hint below.

Serve the mousse with crackers or miniature rye bread.

Serves 12 to 16.

Reminder: Depending on what region of the country you live in, different terms are applied to denote cream. Whipping cream is heavy cream. Table cream is often referred to as light cream or coffee cream, and it will not whip. Half and half, as the name implies, is half milk and half table cream. It can be used in any recipe calling for table cream, without sacrificing texture or flavor.

HINTS

To unmold a congealed mixture, loosen it from the sides and center of the mold with the tip of a small knife. Then quickly dip the bottom of the mold into a bowl or other container of warm—not hot—water. Remove the mold from the water after about 10 seconds to prevent contents from melting. Place a chilled serving plate on top of the mold. Holding both the mold and the plate firmly, invert and shake gently. Carefully lift off the empty mold.

Parsley will keep for a long time in the refrigerator if, after washing it, you place it in a covered jar while it is still slightly damp.

SALMON MOUSSE

Still another molded appetizer that will appeal even to those who profess to dislike salmon. Make at least 4 days ahead of serving.

---

1 can (16 ounces) red salmon + 1 can (7½ ounces) red salmon
1 medium onion, coarsely chopped
½ cup boiling water
1½ tablespoons unflavored gelatin
2 tablespoons lemon juice
½ cup mayonnaise
¼ teaspoon paprika
½ teaspoon dried dill weed, *or* 1 teaspoon fresh dill weed
1 cup light cream

Four days before serving, drain the salmon well and pick out any bits of bone; set aside.

In a blender container, combine the onion, boiling water, gelatin, and lemon juice; blend at high speed for 1 minute.

Add in 3 equal parts, blending well after each addition, the following: mayonnaise, paprika, dill weed, and salmon.

After all the ingredients are well blended, add the cream, one-third at a time.

Lightly oil a 6-cup mold. (A fish-shaped mold is the most appropriate.)

Pour in the salmon mixture, cover with aluminum foil, and refrigerate for 4 days.

Just before serving, unmold the mousse onto a large serving platter. If using a fish-shaped mold, you can decorate the "fish" by using sliced olives for the "eyes" and "scales."

Serve with crackers or miniature rye bread.

Serves 12 to 16.

HOT CRAB SPREAD

Prepare plenty, as this tasty mixture won't last very long!

---

2 packages (8 ounces each) cream cheese, softened
2 tablespoons milk
¼ cup finely chopped onion
   Salt and freshly ground pepper to taste
1 teaspoon chopped parsley
1 can (16 ounces) crab meat, flaked, with all shell and cartilage removed
   Dash of Tabasco sauce
   Dash of Worcestershire sauce
2 tablespoons chopped chives
⅓ cup slivered blanched almonds (optional)

In an ovenproof dish, combine the cream cheese, milk, onion, salt and pepper, parsley, crab meat, Tabasco and Worcestershire sauces, and chives. Blend well.

Bake the mixture at 375 degrees for 15 minutes, or until bubbly.

If using the almonds, sprinkle them over the mixture just before serving.

Keep the crab meat mixture warm in a chafing dish or on an electric hot tray.

Serve with crackers, miniature rye bread, or fresh vegetables.

Serves 6 to 8.

HINT

When a recipe calls for blanched almonds, save money by purchasing whole, unblanched almonds, which are less costly per pound than the blanched variety. To remove the skins, simply pour boiling water over the almonds and let stand for 30 seconds. Drain off the water, and the almond skins will slide right off. Then chop, sliver, or toast, depending on the recipe.

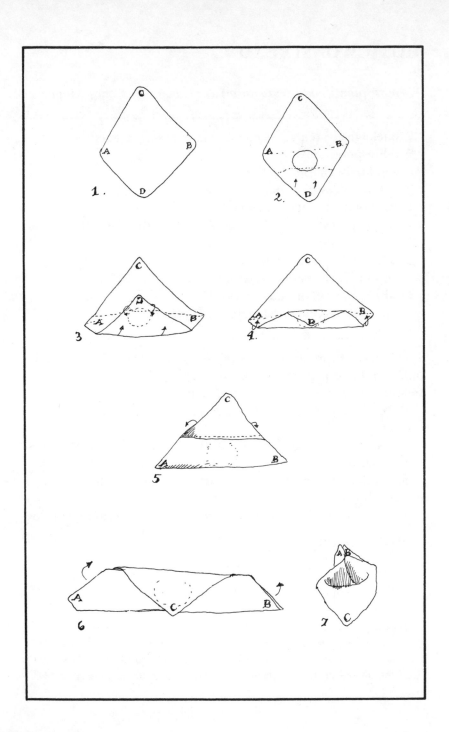

CRAB WONTONS

Wonton wrappers can now be purchased in most supermarkets or Oriental food stores. Or use egg roll wrappers, cut in quarters.

---

2 packages (8 ounces each) cream cheese, softened
1 can (16 ounces) crab meat, flaked, with all shell and car-
    tilage removed
1 teaspoon Worcestershire sauce
⅛ teaspoon Tabasco sauce
    Freshly ground pepper to taste
    Pinch of garlic powder
2 pounds wonton wrappers, or one pound egg roll wrappers,
    cut in quarters
    Oil for deep-frying

In a bowl, combine the cream cheese, crab meat, and Worcestershire and Tabasco sauces, mixing well.

Stir in the pepper and garlic powder to taste.

To assemble the wontons, place a small amount of the filling in the center of each square wonton wrapper.

Fold the wrapper diagonally into a triangle.

Dab a bit of the filling on each side of the mound.

Bring the midpoints of both sides of the triangle together over the exposed filling, and pinch the edges together securely.

Fill a deep-fat fryer or a deep skillet with about 3 inches of oil; heat to 400 degrees. Use a deep-fat thermometer if your utensil is not equipped with one.

Fry wontons until light-golden color. Drain on paper towels, and serve hot.

If not serving wontons right away, cool and place them in a plastic bag or freezer container. To reheat, place frozen wontons on an ungreased cookie sheet, and bake in a 400-degree oven for 7 to 10 minutes.

Makes about 8 dozen.

Cheese

JOSEPHINAS

I brought this delectable recipe back from New Mexico just in time to be the hit at one of my parties.

½ pound butter or margarine, softened
½ teaspoon crushed garlic, *or* ¼ teaspoon garlic powder
2 cans (3½ ounces each) chopped green chilis, drained and with seeds removed
1 cup mayonnaise
½ pound Monterey Jack cheese, grated
2 to 3 packages miniature rye bread, *or* 1 loaf French bread, cut into ¼-inch slices

---

In a small bowl, combine the butter, garlic, and chilis, mixing well.

In another bowl, combine the mayonnaise with the grated cheese.

Preheat the oven to broil.

Place the bread slices on a greased cookie sheet.

Broil the bread, six inches from the heat, on one side only.

Remove the bread from the oven, and turn the slices over. Spread each one with the butter-chili mixture.

Spread the mayonnaise-cheese mixture on top of butter-chili mixture.

Return to oven, and broil, six inches from the heat, until lightly browned and fluffy—about 2 minutes.

Serve immediately, and keep them coming!

Makes 2½ to 3 dozen.

ONION ROUNDS I

⅔ cup mayonnaise
⅓ to ½ cup freshly grated Parmesan cheese
1 small onion, finely chopped
2 to 3 loaves miniature rye or pumpernickel bread
   Paprika

Preheat the oven to broil.

Combine the mayonnaise, Parmesan cheese, and onion.

Spread this mixture on the slices of bread.

Sprinkle the top of each with paprika.

Place the slices on a greased cookie sheet, and broil, six inches from heat, until bubbly. It only takes about a minute, so watch them carefully.

Serve hot. These rounds can be assembled in advance and broiled just before serving.

Makes 2½ to 3 dozen.

HINT

To keep hard cheeses fresh, cover them with a cloth moistened in vinegar; or store the cheese, grated, in a tightly covered jar in the refrigerator.

ONION ROUNDS II

Another savory onion appetizer that also freezes nicely.

---

1 large loaf (22 ounces) soft white bread
2 medium red onions, diced
½ cup mayonnaise
¼ cup grated Parmesan cheese
¼ cup grated Romano cheese
¼ cup chopped parsley

Remove the crusts from the bread, and with a biscuit or cookie cutter, cut each slice into a circle, 2 to 3 inches in diameter. (Save bread scraps for poultry stuffing, bread pudding, or bread crumbs by storing them in a plastic bag in your freezer.)

Sprinkle a small amount of the diced onions on each circle of bread.

In a small bowl, combine the mayonnaise, Parmesan, and Romano cheeses; spread enough of this mixture on each circle to cover the onions.

Sprinkle each circle with the parsley.

Place the rounds on a greased cookie sheet, and bake at 350 degrees for 10 minutes, or until bubbly. Serve hot.

Baked rounds may be frozen and reheated on a cookie sheet at 350 degrees for 15 minutes, or until heated through.

Makes 2½ to 3 dozen.

HINT

If you do not have a round cookie cutter, a glass or a rinsed-out empty soup can is a good substitute, as long as the bread is very soft.

CHILI CON QUESO

A Mexican version of cheese fondue that goes best with corn chips (such as Fritos or Doritos). You can also serve it with raw vegetables or cooked, cold shrimp.

---

2 pounds Velveeta cheese
1 can (10 ounces) prepared enchilada sauce
3 to 4 jalapeno peppers, with seeds removed and finely chopped, *or* 1 can (3½ ounces) chopped green chilis, drained and with seeds removed

---

In a large pot, over very low heat, melt the cheese, stirring frequently.

Stir in the enchilada sauce and the peppers or chilis, mixing woll.

Transfer the mixture to a chafing dish and keep warm while serving.

Makes about 4 cups.

CHEESE PASTRIES

PASTRY:

1 package (8 ounces) cream cheese, softened
½ cup butter, softened
1 cup + 2 tablespoons flour
   Pinch of salt

2 cups grated sharp cheddar cheese

In medium bowl, with an electric mixer at medium speed, cream together the cream cheese and butter until fluffy.

With a wooden spoon, mix in the flour and salt, and gather the dough into a ball.

Wrap the dough in waxed paper, and chill for 1 hour.

Preheat the oven to 375 degrees.

On a lightly floured surface, roll the dough out until it is approximately ⅛-inch thick. (Don't worry if you cannot seem to get it thin enough.)

Using a round biscuit or cookie cutter, cut the dough into circles about 2 inches in diameter.

Place a small amount of grated cheese over each circle.

Fold each circle in half, and crimp the edges together to seal them securely.

Place the pastries on an ungreased cookie sheet and bake for 15 minutes. Serve hot.

Baked pastries can be frozen and reheated on a cookie sheet in a 375-degree oven.

Makes 3 to 4 dozen.

TIROPETES

Assembling these Greek cheese puff triangles may seem tricky at first, but if you imagine the standard way of folding the American flag, it will be easier to visualize—and complete— the process.

---

  1 **pound filo pastry (available at Greek specialty stores)**
  ½ **pound Muenster cheese, grated**
 12 **ounces creamed cottage cheese**
  2 **eggs**
  1 **small onion, grated**
  1 **garlic clove, minced**

2 tablespoons finely chopped parsley
  Salt and freshly ground pepper to taste
1 cup melted butter (Greek butter is best if available)

Unroll the filo pastry and carefully cut it lengthwise into 3 equal portions.

Refrigerate two-thirds of the filo until needed; cover the remaining one-third with a slightly damp towel. (If the towel is too wet it will melt the filo.)

In a bowl combine the cheeses, eggs, onion, garlic, parsley, and salt and pepper.

Remove a sheet of pastry and place it vertically toward you on a flat surface; brush it with a little melted butter.

Fold up about 2 inches of the pastry from the bottom.

Brush this flap with melted butter and place 1 tablespoon of the filling on the bottom right-hand corner of the strip.

Fold the corner from right to left to form a triangle; then fold the corner on the left straight up.

Now fold from left to right. The corner is now on the right, so fold it straight up.

Continue folding in this manner, making sure that the bottom edge, with each fold, is parallel with the alternate-edge side.

Lightly butter the finished triangle.

Repeat this procedure with the remaining dough (including that which you have refrigerated) until all the filling is used up. Any unused filo can be frozen for later use.

Place the triangles on ungreased cookie sheets and bake them at 400 degrees for 15 to 20 minutes, or until they are golden-brown. Serve hot.

The unbaked triangles can also be frozen. To heat, place the triangles directly from the freezer into an oven preheated to 400 degrees, and bake for 25 to 30 minutes, or until they are heated through.

Makes about 6 dozen.

SAGANAKI

Also known as "Flaming Cheese," this brandy-flavored cheese dish will delight your guests.

---

1   pound soft Kasseri or Kefalotiri (available at Greek specialty stores) or mozzarella cheese
2   tablespoons butter
2   tablespoons brandy
1   lemon

Preheat the oven to broil.

Cut the cheese into wedges or bite-sized cubes.

Melt the butter in a butter melter or small saucepan, and brush some on the bottom of a shallow ovenproof pan.

Place the cheese in the pan, and pour the remaining butter over it.

Broil, six inches from heat, until cheese is bubbly and light brown. Remove cheese from the oven.

In a butter melter, over low heat, gently heat the brandy just until warm.

Using a wooden kitchen match, carefully ignite the brandy, and pour it over the hot cheese.

After the flame dies out, squeeze the juice from the lemon over the cheese, and serve immediately, using two spoons to scoop it onto individual plates.

Serves 4 to 6.

HINT

Citrus fruits yield nearly twice the amount of juice if they are dropped into hot water for a few minutes before you squeeze them. Or, you may roll them back and forth beneath your hand on the countertop.

BEER CHEESE

Even non-beer drinkers will enjoy this zesty cheese spread. When packed in an attractive crock or pottery bowl, it makes a nice holiday gift, too.

---

1 pound aged cheddar cheese, finely grated
1 pound Swiss cheese, finely grated
1 garlic clove, mashed
1 teaspoon dry mustard
2 teaspoons Worcestershire sauce
1 cup beer, slightly flat (let stand at room temperature for 1 hour)

Place the cheeses in a large bowl.

Add the garlic, mustard, and Worcestershire sauce.

Using a fork, mix the ingredients until they are well combined.

Gradually add the beer, beating with a wooden spoon until the mixture is blended and of spreading consistency.

Store the mixture in a covered container in the refrigerator until needed.

Serve the cheese at room temperature with miniature rye or pumpernickel bread, or with crackers of your choice.

Serves 20 to 24.

Note: You can also prepare this spread in a food processor or blender, but if you do, you will have to prepare it one-third at a time.

Vegetables

ITALIAN STUFFED MUSHROOMS

---

12 large or 18 medium mushrooms
 4 tablespoons butter
½ teaspoon garlic salt
 2 tablespoons vegetable oil
¼ cup finely chopped shallots or scallions
⅓ cup unseasoned bread crumbs
¼ cup finely chopped baked ham or prosciutto
 3 tablespoons freshly grated Parmesan cheese
 2 tablespoons chopped parsley
   Pinch of oregano
   Salt and freshly ground pepper to taste
 1 to 2 tablespoons Marsala wine

With a mushroom brush or a slightly dampened towel, wipe the mushrooms clean. Remove the stems, chop them finely, and set aside.

In a small skillet, melt 2 tablespoons of butter, and stir in the garlic salt. Remove from the heat.

Brush the mushroom caps with the garlic butter, and place the caps, stem side up, in a shallow baking pan.

In the same skillet, over medium heat, melt 1 tablespoon of butter along with the oil, and sauté the shallots for 1 to 2 minutes, until they are transparent.

Add the chopped mushroom stems, and cook, stirring, for another minute.

Stir in the bread crumbs, ham, cheese, parsley, oregano, and salt and pepper. Remove the pan from the heat.

Add the Marsala a little at a time, using only enough to slightly moisten the mixture.

Spoon the mixture into the mushroom caps.

Melt the remaining tablespoon of butter, and sprinkle a few drops over each mushroom.

Bake at 350 degrees for 15 to 20 minutes, or until the stuffing is lightly browned. Serve immediately.

Makes 12 to 18.

HINTS

When buying mushrooms, select those that are firm, white to creamy in color and that have closed caps. The gills should not be showing; if they are, the mushrooms are old and tired.

One pound of whole mushrooms equals about 12 to 15 large mushrooms, or 25 to 30 medium mushrooms, or 36 to 45 small (or button) mushrooms.

One pound of fresh mushrooms (uncooked) will yield about 5 cups sliced.

When cleaning mushrooms, never immerse them in water. Mushrooms are like sponges, and you will never be able to get rid of the excess water they absorb. It is best to use a special soft-bristled mushroom brush or a slightly dampened towel to clean them.

MUSHROOM CROUSTADES

One of my most requested recipes; it will be one of yours, too!

CROUSTADES:

2 tablespoons butter or margarine, softened
24 slices soft, thinly sliced white bread

FILLING:

½ pound fresh mushrooms
¼ cup butter
3 tablespoons finely chopped shallots
2 tablespoons flour
1 cup heavy cream
   Salt and freshly ground pepper to taste
   Pinch of cayenne pepper
1 tablespoon finely chopped parsley
1½ tablespoons finely chopped chives
½ teaspoon lemon juice
3 tablespoons grated Parmesan cheese
   Additional butter for topping

With the softened butter, coat the insides of 24 3-inch muffin tins.

Remove the crusts from the bread and cut each slice into a 3-inch round, using a cookie cutter. (Freeze the bread scraps for future use.)

Carefully place the bread rounds into the greased tins, molding them to the shape of the tins to form little cups.

Bake the croustades at 400 degrees for 10 minutes, or until lightly browned.

Remove the croustades from the tins, and set aside to fill later; or cool and freeze in a large plastic bag until needed.

To make the filling, wipe the mushrooms clean, and chop them very finely.

Melt the butter in a large skillet, over medium heat, and add the chopped shallots. Cook, stirring, for 3 minutes.

Add the chopped mushrooms and continue cooking, stirring occasionally, for about 15 minutes, or until all the moisture has evaporated.

Remove the skillet from the heat, and stir in the flour, blending well.

Add the cream to this mixture, return the skillet to medium heat, and bring to a boil, stirring constantly.

As the mixture thickens, turn the heat down to low, and cook another minute or two, to remove the taste of the flour.

Remove the pan from the heat, and add the seasonings, herbs, and lemon juice.

Place the mixture in a bowl to cool. The entire recipe may be assembled in advance up to this point.

About 15 minutes before serving, fill the croustades with the mushroom filling, sprinkle with the Parmesan cheese, and dot with additional butter.

Place the croustades on an ungreased cookie sheet, and bake at 350 degrees for 10 minutes. Serve immediately.

Makes 2 dozen.

MARINATED MUSHROOMS

1 pound small mushrooms
2 cups water
4 cups white vinegar (approx.)
½ cup olive oil
4 garlic cloves, slivered
2 teaspoons salt
1 teaspoon whole peppercorns

Wipe the mushrooms clean with a brush or dampened towel.
Place them in a large stainless-steel or enamel saucepan.
Add the water and 2 cups of the vinegar.
Bring the liquid to a boil over high heat; lower the heat, and simmer the mushrooms for five minutes.
Drain the mushrooms in a colander, discarding the cooking liquid.
In a large jar or refrigerator dish, mix the olive oil, slivered garlic, salt, and peppercorns.
Add the mushrooms to this mixture, and pour in enough of the remaining white vinegar to cover them completely.
Store the mushrooms, tightly covered, in the refrigerator several hours or overnight.
Drain off the marinade just before serving, being careful to remove any peppercorns that might get lodged in the mushrooms.
Serve the mushrooms speared with toothpicks.

Serves 4.

DRUNKEN TOMATOES

This is not really a recipe, but a sure-fire combination to bowl over your guests!

---

1 pint cherry tomatoes
1 cup vodka
1 cup rock salt or Kosher salt

Wash the tomatoes, and remove the stems.

Fill a decorative glass or crystal bowl with ice cubes, and place the tomatoes on top of the ice.

Place the vodka in another smaller bowl and the salt in a third.

To serve, spear a tomato with a toothpick, dip it in the vodka and then in the salt . . . and enjoy!

Serves 4 to 6.

ASPARAGUS ROLLUPS

Even my nine-year-old son (who hates asparagus) asks me to fix these!

---

20 slices very soft white bread, with crusts removed
 1 package (8 ounces) cream cheese, softened
 4 ounces bleu cheese, crumbled
 1 egg
   Dash of Tabasco sauce
   Dash of Worcestershire sauce

1 can (14½ ounces) asparagus spears, well drained
½ cup melted butter or margarine

Flatten the bread out by rolling each slice once or twice with a rolling pin.

In a small bowl, combine the cheeses, egg, and Tabasco and Worcestershire sauces.

Spread this mixture evenly on each slice of bread.

Place one asparagus spear on each slice of bread, and roll up. If the spears are longer than the slices of bread, trim off the "overhang," and use 3 or 4 such extra pieces to fill one slice of bread.

Dip each piece of the rolled-up bread in the melted butter, and slice into thirds. If not serving right away, rollups can be frozen at this point and reheated using the regular baking directions below.

Place the slices on an ungreased cookie sheet.

Bake the rollups at 425 degrees for 15 minutes, or until golden. Serve hot.

Makes 5 dozen.

HINT

To preserve the flavor of Tabasco sauce, store it in the refrigerator.

ARTICHOKE NIBBLERS

A unique appetizer for any get-together. They taste best when served hot.

---

2 jars (6 ounces each) marinated artichoke hearts
1 small onion, finely chopped
2 garlic cloves, finely chopped
4 eggs
¼ cup unseasoned bread crumbs
  Salt and freshly ground pepper to taste
⅛ teaspoon oregano
  Dash of Tabasco sauce to taste
2 cups grated sharp cheddar cheese
2 tablespoons finely chopped parsley

Drain the marinade from one of the jars of artichokes, and place the liquid in a skillet. Drain the other jar, discarding the liquid.

Finely chop the artichoke hearts, and set aside.

Heat the artichoke liquid, and sauté the onion and garlic for 3 minutes; remove from the heat.

In a large bowl, beat the eggs well.

Add the bread crumbs, salt, pepper, oregano, and Tabasco sauce to the eggs, mixing well.

Stir in the cheese, parsley, artichokes, and the onion mixture.

Grease a 9 × 9 × 2-inch baking pan, and pour in the mixture.

Bake at 325 degrees for 30 minutes. Cut into small squares. Serve immediately.

The squares can be refrigerated for future use and served cold or reheated at 325 degrees for 10 to 12 minutes.

Makes about 3 dozen.

Reminder: *One pound of hard cheese (Cheddar, Swiss, Monterey Jack, or Parmesan) yields 4 cups of grated cheese.*

ARTICHOKE HEARTS IN PATTY SHELLS

This dish broke up a friendship; one friend would not give the other the recipe!

---

1 package (6) frozen patty shells
2 packages (3 ounces each) cream cheese and chives, softened
2 tablespoons butter or margarine, softened
1 egg
4 to 6 drops Tabasco sauce
⅛ teaspoon Worcestershire sauce
  Freshly ground pepper to taste
¼ teaspoon garlic powder
6 artichoke hearts packed in water (not marinade)

Bake the patty shells according to the package directions. Remove the inner circle, and hollow out the shells. Set aside to cool.

In a medium bowl, with an electric mixer at medium speed, cream the cream cheese and chives with the butter.

Add the egg, beating well.

Add the Tabasco and Worcestershire sauces, pepper, and garlic powder, beating until all the ingredients are well mixed.

Place a spoonful of the cream cheese mixture in the bottom of each patty shell.

Place an artichoke heart on top of the cream cheese mixture, and cover each heart with another spoonful of mixture.

The recipe may be made in advance and refrigerated at this point.

Place the patty shells on an ungreased cookie sheet, and bake at 375 degrees for 10 minutes, or until the cream cheese mixture is bubbly.

Serve hot on small individual plates.

Serves 6.

Dips

Many people rebel against serving dips to company because they seem so hackneyed. But, let's face it; dips are very much a part of informal entertaining in America.

And they need not be dull, as the following recipes demonstrate. Two additional advantages of serving dips are that they are incredibly easy to prepare, and they lend themselves to all sorts of accompaniments—from raw vegetables to cold shrimp to crackers to corn chips.

GREEN GODDESS DIP

2 soft, ripe avocados, peeled and mashed
2 cups sour cream
½ cup mayonnaise
½ teaspoon salt
¾ cup finely chopped parsley
¼ cup chopped scallions (including some of the green tops)

Place the mashed avocados in a refrigerator dish, and mix in the sour cream, mayonnaise, and salt.

Fold in the parsley and chopped scallions.

Cover, and refrigerate until serving.

Makes about 3 cups.

To Save Calories: *Mock sour cream can be made by combining 1 pound of cottage cheese in the blender with 2 tablespoons of lemon juice and a pinch of salt. Blend the mixture* *until very smooth. It will not be as tart as sour cream, but the texture should be comparable. Once flavored with other ingredients, mock sour cream will taste almost as good as the real thing.*

BENEDICTINE DIP

---

1 medium cucumber
2 packages (3 ounces each) cream cheese, softened
1 tablespoon grated onion
  Dash of Tabasco sauce
2 to 3 tablespoons mayonnaise
1 tablespoon Benedictine (or brandy)
  Salt to taste

Peel the cucumber, and cut in half lengthwise.

With a spoon, scoop out the seeds, and discard.

Using a food processor or a hand grater, finely grate the cucumber.

Place the grated cucumber in a refrigerator dish, and add the remaining ingredients, mixing well.

Cover, and chill until serving.

Makes about 1 cup.

CURRY DIP

A delicious dip for raw vegetables or shrimp.

---

2 cups mayonnaise
3 tablespoons chili sauce

1 tablespoon curry powder
  Salt and freshly ground pepper to taste
1 tablespoon garlic powder
1 tablespoon grated onion
1 tablespoon Worcestershire sauce

Combine all the ingredients in a refrigerator dish.
Cover, and chill until serving.
This mixture will keep for several weeks in the refrigerator.

Makes about 2½ cups.

SPINACH DIP

1 cup mayonnaise
1 cup sour cream
1 package (10 ounces) frozen chopped spinach, defrosted
    and well drained
  Salt and freshly ground pepper to taste
½ cup finely chopped parsley
½ cup grated onion

The day before serving, combine all the ingredients in a
refrigerator dish, mixing well.
Cover, and chill overnight.
This dip tastes best when served with raw vegetables.

Makes 3 cups.

HINT

As with all herbs, fresh parsley is preferable to the dried
variety, but if you must use the latter, remember that it is
more concentrated. Therefore, use only half the amount of
parsley called for in any given recipe.

Soups

SPINACH EGG-DROP SOUP

Also called Stracciatella or "Rags" Soup.

3½ cups fresh or canned chicken broth
  1 package (10 ounces) frozen chopped spinach
  1 egg
 ¼ cup freshly grated Parmesan cheese
    Freshly ground pepper to taste

In a large saucepan, bring 1 cup of the chicken broth to a boil, and add the spinach.

Cover the saucepan, and cook over high heat until the spinach is bright green and well cooked.

With a slotted spoon, remove the spinach from the broth, and set aside.

Add the remaining broth to the saucepan, and bring to a boil.

In a small bowl, beat the egg lightly, then beat in the grated cheese.

When the broth is boiling, pour in the egg-cheese mixture, stirring constantly.

Add the spinach and pepper. Cook for another minute, and serve immediately.

Serves 6 to 8.

GAZPACHO

A cold soup of Spanish origin that is ideal for warm-weather entertaining.

```
  3 tomatoes, peeled and chopped
  1 large cucumber, peeled and chopped
  1 large onion, finely chopped
  1 green pepper, seeded and chopped
2½ cups tomato juice
 11 tablespoons olive oil
  7 tablespoons red wine vinegar
    Dash of Tabasco sauce
    Salt and freshly ground pepper to taste
  3 garlic cloves, peeled and halved
  3 thin slices white bread, with crusts removed, cut in cubes
```

Several hours before serving, combine 2 of the chopped tomatoes, half the cucumber, and half the onion with the chopped green pepper in a large bowl.

Add about ¾ cup of the tomato juice.

Place one-half of the mixture in a blender container, and blend at high speed for 1 minute to purée the vegetables. Repeat with the other half.

Return the puréed mixture to the bowl, and, using a wire whisk, mix the purée with the remaining tomato juice, 9 tablespoons of olive oil, the vinegar, Tabasco sauce, salt, and pepper.

Refrigerate this mixture, covered, until well chilled—at least 3 hours.

In a small skillet, heat the remaining 2 tablespoons of olive oil over medium-low heat. Sauté the garlic and bread cubes until crisp and golden.

Drain the bread cubes well on a paper towel. Set the garlic aside to cool.

Crush the cooled garlic and add to the chilled soup.

To serve, ladle the chilled soup into a tureen. Arrange the reserved chopped vegetables and the croutons in small bowls, and serve along with the soup to be sprinkled on top of each serving. Chopped hard-boiled eggs can also be used as a garnish.

Serves 6.

HINTS

To peel a tomato easily, spear it with a kitchen fork and plunge it in boiling water for 30 seconds. Remove it from the water, and the skin will slide right off.

A pinch is slightly more than a dash. In general, a pinch refers to dried seasonings (salt, pepper, herbs, etc.), and a dash refers to liquid ingredients (Worcestershire, Tabasco). Occasionally, however, a recipe will call for a dash of salt. These minute quantities are indicated whenever the given ingredient has a distinct flavor that can affect the final product if added too heavily. So add just a little, and then taste to see if you want to increase the quantity. Do not go overboard!

THE BEST ONION SOUP

Wherein the lowly onion is transformed into a grand gastro-nomic experience! Serve before a light main course, or as a late-evening meal in itself.

¼ pound butter
1 pound Spanish onions, very thinly sliced
1 heaping tablespoon flour
3 cups fresh or canned chicken broth
1 fifth of good champagne, well chilled
  Salt and freshly ground pepper to taste
  Pinch of cayenne pepper
10 thin slices stale French bread
1 cup grated Gruyère cheese

In a large skillet, melt the butter, and add the onion slices, separating the rings with a fork.

Cook, stirring, until all the rings are coated with butter.

Continue cooking until the onions are soft and golden-brown.

Sprinkle the flour, salt, and pepper to taste, and the pinch of cayenne pepper over the onions, and cook for 2 to 3 minutes, stirring constantly, until the flour browns lightly.

Meanwhile, in a small saucepan heat the broth to a boil, and add to the onions.

Bring the mixture to a boil; lower the heat, and simmer 15 minutes. The mixture may be made in advance and refrigerated up to this point.

About 20 minutes before serving, transfer the onion soup to a large kettle, and add the champagne. A whole bottle of champagne will produce a thin soup; if you desire a thicker consistency, use less champagne.

Stir to blend well, and simmer over low heat.

Arrange the bread slices on an ungreased cookie sheet, and bake at 250 degrees until they are crisp and lightly browned, turning once.

Turn the oven heat up to broil.

Arrange the bread slices in the bottom of a large casserole in one or two layers. Sprinkle half of the grated cheese over the bread.

Pour the soup over the bread, and cover with the remaining grated cheese.

Broil six inches from heat just long enough to melt the cheese and brown the top lightly. Serve immediately.

Serves 6 to 8.

─────────── **HINT** ───────────

Wine used in cooking acts as a seasoning only since the alcohol evaporates during cooking, leaving the wine essence, which provides the flavor. For this reason, you should use only good wines in cooking.

CANTALOUPE SOUP

Cantaloupe is one of the most nutritious and low-calorie fruits available. When you tire of serving it plain or in salads, here is a different way to use it.

---

1 cantaloupe (about 3 pounds), peeled, seeded and cut into 1-inch cubes
½ cup champagne, or more
2 tablespoons sugar
1 tablespoon lime juice
  Mint leaves for garnish

Place the cubes of cantaloupe in a food processor or blender container.

Add the champagne, sugar, and lime juice and blend until smooth.

Pour the soup into a serving bowl and refrigerate, covered, for at least 3 hours.

To serve, spoon the soup into individual soup cups and garnish with mint leaves.

Serves 4 to 6.

LEMON SOUP

Easy and impressive.

---

6 cups fresh or canned chicken broth
3 tablespoons uncooked long-grain white rice
3 eggs
3 tablespoons lemon juice

In a medium saucepan over medium heat cook the broth and the rice for 15 to 20 minutes.

In a small bowl, beat the eggs lightly, and gradually add the lemon juice, beating continuously.

Pour a small amount of the hot soup into the egg mixture; then return this mixture to the soup in the saucepan.

Do not heat any further. If the eggs begin to curdle, beat the soup with a wire whisk. Serve at once.

Serves 6.

CREAM OF ALMOND SOUP

---

2 tablespoons flour
1 tablespoon butter
1 tablespoon potato starch
4½ cups fresh or canned chicken broth
½ teaspoon salt
¼ teaspoon dried mustard
   Pinch of mace
⅛ teaspoon powdered ginger
2 garlic cloves

1 lemon slice
  Freshly ground pepper to taste
  Pinch of cayenne pepper
1 cup finely ground blanched almonds
½ to 1 cup heavy cream

Place the flour, butter, and potato starch in a large bowl. Cream until the flour and potato starch are thoroughly incorporated into the butter. Form into a ball, and set the bowl aside.

Heat the chicken broth in a medium saucepan.

Add 1 cup of the broth to the butter mixture, stirring constantly; then add the remaining hot broth to the bowl, stirring constantly.

Stir in the salt, mustard, mace, ginger, garlic, and lemon slice.

Return this mixture to the saucepan, and bring to a boil, still stirring; reduce the heat, and simmer 5 to 10 minutes.

Remove the garlic cloves and the lemon slice, and discard.

Add the pepper and cayenne to the soup.

Stir in the almonds, and simmer another 2 minutes.

Add ½ cup of cream to the soup. If you desire a richer soup, add the remaining ½ cup.

Bring the mixture just to the boiling point, and serve at once.

Serves 6 to 8.

Chapter 2
MAIN DISHES

Beef
Veal
Pork & Lamb
Chicken
Fish & Seafood
Meatless

Beef

STIR-FRIED BEEF AND VEGETABLES

Although this dish cannot be prepared in advance, it is simple to assemble quickly if all your ingredients are ready. Use a wok to prepare this tasty, low-calorie dish.

MARINADE:

¼ cup soy sauce
2 garlic cloves, finely chopped
½ teaspoon powdered ginger
   Pinch of MSG (optional)

BEEF and VEGETABLES:

1½ pounds of round steak, sliced paper-thin
    Peanut oil
1 teaspoon cornstarch
½ cup water
1 teaspoon soy sauce
   Freshly ground pepper to taste
2 pounds fresh spinach, washed, drained, and chopped
½ pound mushrooms, wiped clean and sliced
1 can (8½ ounces) bamboo shoots, drained

To make the marinade, combine the soy sauce, garlic, ginger, and the optional MSG in a medium bowl.

Add the meat, mixing to coat it well with the marinade. Refrigerate, covered, for several hours or overnight.

About 15 minutes before serving, drain the meat, reserving the marinade.

Heat a tablespoon of peanut oil in a wok over medium heat.

Add the meat, a handful at a time, stirring until it is browned on all sides; push the meat up the sides of the wok as it cooks, and continue cooking the remaining meat in this fashion.

Remove the meat from the wok, and keep it warm.

Combine the cornstarch, water, soy sauce, and pepper to taste with the reserved marinade.

Pour this mixture into the wok, and cook, stirring constantly, until it thickens. Pour the sauce over the meat.

Heat another tablespoon of oil in the wok, and stir in the spinach. Cook the spinach for 2 to 3 minutes, and push it up the sides of the wok.

Add a little more oil, if needed, and quickly cook the mushrooms and bamboo shoots.

Return the meat and sauce to the wok, and stir everything together, cooking only until the meat is heated through.

Serve immediately with boiled white rice or Chinese Oven Rice. (See recipe on page 137.)

Serves 4 to 6.

Note: Other fresh or canned vegetables can be added along with —or instead of—the mushrooms and bamboo shoots. Suggested vegetables are sliced celery, chopped onions, fresh or canned bean sprouts, snow peas, or water chestnuts.

CHINESE STEAK WITH PEA PODS

Like most Oriental dishes, this one is short on calories but long on flavor.

1 pound flank steak
3 tablespoons hoisin sauce (available at Oriental specialty stores)
2 tablespoons soy sauce

1 teaspoon sesame seed oil (available at specialty stores)
2 teaspoons cornstarch
½ teaspoon garlic powder
3 to 4 thin slices fresh ginger root, finely chopped (or use powdered ginger to taste)
  Peanut oil
1 package (10 ounces) frozen Chinese pea pods, defrosted and drained
½ pound mushrooms, sliced (optional)
2 firm tomatoes, cut into wedges

Slice the meat into thin strips, about ½-inch wide by 1½-inches long.

In a small bowl combine the hoisin, soy sauce, the sesame seed oil, cornstarch, garlic powder, and ginger.

Add the meat to the sauce and stir well, coating each piece.

Heat 2 to 3 tablespoons of peanut oil in a wok over medium heat.

Add half of the meat; cook, stirring constantly, until meat is cooked—about 3 minutes. Remove the meat to a platter.

Add more oil to the wok, if necessary, and cook the remaining meat; remove it to the platter with the other meat.

Add the pea pods and the optional mushrooms to the wok and cook, stirring, for 1 minute.

Return the meat to the wok, along with the tomato wedges. Stir everything together and cook just long enough to heat the tomatoes.

Serve immediately over boiled white rice.

Serves 4 to 6.

HINT

To slice the beef paper-thin, you should freeze it slightly first.

MARINATED STEAK KABOBS

This marinade recipe will enhance any kind of meat for indoor or outdoor cooking.

MARINADE:

    Salt and freshly ground pepper to taste
2 tablespoons soy sauce
1 teaspoon garlic powder, or to taste
¼ cup catsup
2 tablespoons vegetable oil
1½ teaspoons Worcestershire sauce
1½ teaspoons dry mustard

KABOBS:

1 to 2 pounds round or chuck steak, cut into 1-inch cubes
1 can (4 ounces) button mushrooms, drained
1 green pepper, cut into 1-inch squares
1 large onion, cut into wedges
16 to 20 cherry tomatoes
1 can (15 ounces) pineapple chunks, drained

To make the marinade, combine the salt, pepper, soy sauce, garlic powder, catsup, oil, Worcestershire sauce, and dry mustard in a medium bowl, mixing well.

Add the meat, and marinate it in this mixture in the refrigerator for several hours or overnight. Turn the meat every few hours.

About 15 minutes before serving, preheat the oven to broil.

Drain the meat, reserving the marinade.

Thread the meat on bamboo skewers alternately with the vegetables and pineapple.

Brush the vegetables, the pineapple, and the meat with the reserved marinade.

Place the skewers on a rack over a shallow baking dish, and

broil them, six inches from the heat, for about 5 minutes on each side. The kabobs can also be barbecued directly over hot coals.

Serve the kabobs on their skewers over a bed of beef-flavored rice, or any boiled rice dish.

Serves 4 to 6.

BUFFET SURPRISE

One of my favorite party/buffet dishes. It can be made up to one week in advance and refrigerated; the longer it sits, the better it gets! It can also be frozen and reheated. Everybody loves it!

---

1 3-pound boneless chuck roast or chuck steak
3 cans (27 ounces each) sauerkraut, drained
1 box (1 pound) brown sugar
1 can (28 ounces) whole tomatoes, with the liquid
1 whole large onion, peeled
1 apple, cored, peeled, and sliced
   Fresh ground pepper

Place the meat in a large kettle or Dutch oven.
Place the drained sauerkraut on top of the meat.
Empty the box of brown sugar into the kettle.
Pour the can of tomatoes over this mixture.
Add the onion, pepper, and the apple slices.
Cover the pot, and simmer over low heat until the meat falls apart when gently poked with a fork—about 4 hours.

Serve hot with buttered noodles or potatoes, or refrigerate the mixture until needed. One advantage of precooking and refrigerating this dish is that you will be able to skim off the fat before you reheat it.

Serves 6 to 8.

Know Your Apples: *Winesap is an all-purpose variety, as are McIntosh, Stayman, and Jonathan. Rome Beauty apples are best for baking, while Delicious apples should be eaten fresh or used in salads.*

HINT

If you want to make economy cuts of beef more tender, you can do so by grinding, cubing, scoring, or pounding the meat to break up the connective tissue. A marinade containing oil and/or vinegar or lemon juice will also help to tenderize the meat.

BEEF ROULADES

A very filling dish that only requires a simple salad or green vegetable as an accompaniment.

CRÊPE BATTER:

1½ cups milk
3 eggs
1½ cups flour
   Pinch of salt
1 teaspoon melted butter
   Additional melted butter

FILLING:

3 tablespoons butter
¾ to 1 pound ground chuck
1 medium onion, finely chopped
¾ pound mushrooms, wiped clean and finely chopped
   Pinch of salt
2 garlic cloves, crushed
1½ teaspoons dry mustard
1 tablespoon bottled steak sauce
½ cup catsup
1 tablespoon chopped parsley
1 teaspoon oregano
1 bay leaf, crumbled
¼ teaspoon rosemary
2 cups crumbled cheddar cheese
½ cup grated Parmesan cheese

TOPPING:

½ cup grated Parmesan cheese
16 slices mozzarella cheese (about 1 pound)
   Paprika

To make the crêpes, put the milk and eggs in a blender container.

Add the flour, salt, and 1 teaspoon of butter, and blend well. If possible, allow the batter to sit for an hour at room temperature before using it.

Heat a 7- or 8-inch crêpe pan over medium heat for a few minutes, and brush the pan with a little melted butter.

Pour in enough crêpe batter just to cover the bottom of the pan (about 3 tablespoons).

Cook the crêpe until it is dry on the top and lightly browned on the bottom. Turn the crêpe, and brown it lightly on the other side.

Remove the crêpe from the pan and place on wire rack, and repeat the process. Makes about 15 crêpes.

If you are not filling the crêpes right away, keep them moist by covering them with a dampened tea towel.

To make the filling, melt the butter in a large skillet, and brown the meat, onion, and mushrooms.

Add the remaining filling ingredients, and simmer the mixture, covered, over low heat until the cheese has melted. Remove from the heat.

Spread a few tablespoons of the filling on each crêpe. Fold the crêpe in thirds, and place it, seam side down, in a buttered shallow baking dish.

Cover the crêpes with the topping ingredients: Sprinkle them first with the Parmesan; then lay the slices of mozzarella cheese over the crêpes, and sprinkle liberally with the paprika. At this point the dish can be covered and refrigerated or frozen until needed.

Bake at 350 degrees for 30 minutes, or until the cheese on top has melted.

Serves 6 to 8.

POOR MAN'S LASAGNE

This casserole is somewhat similar to lasagne, but it's easier to assemble, slightly less costly, and just as flavorful.

½ pound broad egg noodles
1 pound ground beef
  Salt and freshly ground pepper to taste
2 cups fresh or canned tomato sauce
  Pinch of basil
  Pinch of oregano
1 cup creamed cottage cheese
½ cup sour cream
1½ cups grated cheddar cheese
¼ cup minced scallions (including some of the green tops)

Prepare the noodles according to the package directions. Drain well, and set aside.

In a large skillet, brown the beef in its own fat until no traces of red show.

Season with salt and pepper.

Add the tomato sauce and herbs; simmer over low heat for 10 minutes.

In a small bowl, combine the cottage cheese, sour cream, cheddar cheese, and scallions.

Place half of the noodles in a buttered 2-quart casserole, and top with half of the cheese mixture. Repeat, using the remaining noodles and cheese mixture.

Pour the meat sauce over all. The dish can be assembled in advance up to this point and refrigerated or frozen until needed.

Bake at 375 degrees for 45 minutes (longer if frozen).

Serves 4 to 6.

BOEUF BOURGUIGNON

This perennially popular French-style beef stew is perfect for fall and winter entertaining. It can (and should) be made several days in advance because the flavor improves with age. Serve it with buttered, parslied potatoes or noodles, as well as French bread and a green salad. For drinking, buy an additional bottle of the wine you use to cook the casserole. (This, by the way, is a good rule of thumb for almost any main dish made with wine.)

---

3 pounds stewing beef, cut into 1-inch cubes
½ cup flour, seasoned with salt and pepper
¼ cup bacon grease (approx.)
2 tablespoons brandy
1 pound whole small white onions, *or* 2 cans (16 ounces each) white onions, well drained
¾ pound small whole mushrooms, wiped clean
3 cups red Burgundy wine
2 beef bouillon cubes
1 bay leaf

Drain the beef cubes on paper towels. Dredge them in the seasoned flour.

In a large kettle or Dutch oven, heat the bacon grease over medium-high heat. (Butter or oil can be substituted, but the bacon grease provides a more full-bodied flavor.)

Brown the meat, a few cubes at a time, adding more grease as needed.

Remove the meat as it browns, and keep it warm.

When all the meat has been browned, return it to the kettle over low heat.

Gently heat the brandy in a butter melter; ignite it with a wooden kitchen match, and pour it over the beef.

When the flame dies out, remove the beef from the kettle, and set it aside.

Over medium heat, melt a little more bacon grease in the kettle, and add the onions (if using fresh onions, see the hint below) and the mushrooms. Cook, stirring occasionally, until the onions are nicely browned.

Place the beef, onions, and mushrooms in a 3- or 4-quart casserole.

Add the wine, beef bouillon cubes, and bay leaf. Cover the casserole.

Bake the casserole at 300 degrees for 2 to 3 hours, or until the meat is tender.

If the sauce gets too thick, add a little more wine. If it is too thin, reduce it by removing the cover during the last hour of cooking. In either case, check the casserole about every half-hour.

The casserole can be served immediately (discard the bay leaf before serving), or it can be refrigerated for later use.

If you refrigerate the casserole, let it warm up to room temperature for a few hours before reheating it. Then bake at 300 degrees for 45 minutes to 1 hour.

Serves 6 to 8.

HINTS

If using fresh white onions, you can peel them easily by plunging them in boiling water for 2 minutes; drain off the water, and when the onions are cool enough to handle, pare away the stem ends, and slide the skins off.

Whenever you cook bacon, drain the grease into a glass or metal container and refrigerate it for use in recipes such as the one above.

BEEF OR LAMB WITH OYSTER SAUCE

For a quick company dish, this one is easy to fix and divine to eat. Oyster sauce can be purchased in Oriental specialty stores.

¼ cup soy sauce
1 tablespoon sugar
¼ cup oyster sauce
2 pounds round steak or lamb shoulder, thinly sliced
2 teaspoons cornstarch
¼ cup vegetable oil
1 bunch scallions, chopped into ½-inch-long strips (including some of the green tops)
1 tablespoon dry cocktail sherry
¼ teaspoon finely chopped fresh ginger, *or* ½ teaspoon powdered ginger
2 dashes of Tabasco sauce

In a medium bowl, combine the soy sauce, sugar, and 2 tablespoons of the oyster sauce.

Marinate the meat in this mixture for at least 1 hour.

Stir in the cornstarch until well blended.

Heat the oil in a wok, and add the meat (along with the marinade), a handful at a time. Stir the meat quickly over high heat until it is well done; it only takes a few minutes.

As the meat cooks, push it up the sides of the wok, and add more meat. Add more oil as needed, letting it heat up before adding more meat.

Add the remaining 2 tablespoons of oyster sauce, the scallions, sherry, ginger, and Tabasco sauce. Stir well, and cook for a minute or two.

Serve hot, with boiled white rice.

Serves 4 to 6.

Veal

VEAL ROLLATINI

An Italian variation of Veal Cordon Bleu. Any rice dish will go perfectly with this delicious dish. You can also serve your favorite variety of pasta, tossed lightly in butter.

---

10 small veal scallops (each about 6 × 3 inches and ¼-inch thick)
10 slices prosciutto or baked ham
10 slices Swiss cheese
 1 package (10 ounces) frozen chopped spinach, thawed and well drained
½ cup Italian flavored bread crumbs
¼ cup butter or margarine
 3 tablespoons flour
 2 cups fresh or canned beef bouillon
   Salt and freshly ground pepper to taste
⅓ cup dry red wine
   Oregano

Lay each slice of veal between two sheets of waxed paper, and flatten it with a rolling pin. Remove the veal from the waxed paper.

On each piece of veal, place a slice of ham and a slice of cheese.

In the middle of the cheese, place about a tablespoon of the thawed spinach.

Roll up the scallops, and secure them with wooden toothpicks.

Dredge the rolls in the bread crumbs.

Melt the butter in a large skillet, and brown the veal rolls on all sides.

Transfer the rolls to a shallow baking dish.

With a wire whisk, stir flour into the butter remaining in the skillet.

Add the beef bouillon, salt, and pepper to taste, and cook the sauce over low heat, stirring constantly, for about 10 minutes, or until it has thickened.

Remove the pan from the heat, and stir in the wine.

Pour the sauce over the veal rolls, and sprinkle a little oregano on top.

The dish may be prepared in advance up to this point.

Bake the veal rolls, uncovered, at 350 degrees for 30 minutes.

Remove the toothpicks just before serving.

Serves 4 to 6.

VEAL AND MUSHROOMS IN SOUR CREAM SAUCE

12 **veal scallops (each about 8 × 3 inches and ½-inch thick)**
   Salt and freshly ground pepper to taste
½ **cup flour**
 6 **to 8 tablespoons butter**
 1 **cup finely chopped onion**
 1 **pound mushrooms, wiped clean and sliced**
¼ **cup brandy**
 1 **cup sour cream**
½ **teaspoon salt**

Dry the veal well, and sprinkle it with salt and pepper.

Dredge the veal in the flour.

In a large skillet, melt 2 tablespoons of the butter until it is bubbly, and add the veal scallops, a few at a time; add more butter as needed. Do not crowd the veal.

Cook the veal about 3 minutes on each side. Remove each scallop as it browns, and place it on a warm platter.

Melt 2 more tablespoons of butter, and sauté the onion for 3 minutes, stirring with a wooden spoon.

Add 2 more tablespoons of butter, and stir in the mushrooms with the onions. Cover the skillet, and let the vegetables cook over low heat for 5 to 8 minutes, or until tender. Stir occasionally.

Add the brandy. Shake the skillet carefully to ignite the brandy, but if it does not catch fire, ignite it with a wooden kitchen match.

Let the flame subside, and stir in the sour cream and salt. Bring to a boil, and correct the seasonings.

Return the veal to the skillet, spoon the sauce over it, and bring the sauce to the boiling point, but do not let it boil.

Serve the veal immediately with buttered noodles.

Serves 6 to 8.

ESCALOPES DE VEAU NORMANDE

The Normandy region of France is noted for its Calvados, or apple brandy.

---

 3 sweet apples, peeled and chopped
     Juice of 2 lemons
14 veal scallops (about ¼-inch thick)
     Salt and freshly ground pepper to taste
½ cup flour
 6 tablespoons butter
 2 tablespoons vegetable oil
⅓ cup Calvados or Applejack
1½ cups heavy cream

Place the apples in a bowl, and pour the lemon juice over them; set aside.

Season the veal with salt and pepper to taste, and dredge the scallops in the flour. Shake off any excess.

Heat the butter and oil in a large, heavy skillet, and brown the veal, a few pieces at a time, on both sides; do not crowd the veal. Remove the pieces of veal as they brown, and keep them warm.

To the same skillet, add the apples, lemon juice, and Calvados or Applejack.

With a wire whisk, scrape up any pieces of flour that have stuck to the skillet, and cook the mixture over medium heat, stirring constantly, for 3 minutes.

Add the cream, and continue cooking until it is well blended into the sauce.

Reduce the heat, and simmer the mixture until it is reduced by one-half and coats a wooden spoon. Correct the seasonings.

Return the veal to the skillet, spooning the sauce over the meat. Leave the veal in the skillet just long enough to heat it through.

Serve hot, with boiled white rice.

Serves 4 to 6.

Pork and Lamb

PORK AND PRUNES À LA LOIRE

An unusual main dish that is quite rich; French bread and a green salad will suffice as accompaniments. Serve this dish with the same wine as you use in the recipe.

---

30 pitted prunes
 2 cups white wine (Vouvray is best.)
 3 pounds boneless fresh pork tenderloin
⅓ cup flour
 6 tablespoons butter
   Salt and freshly ground pepper to taste
 1 tablespoon red currant jelly
 1 cup heavy cream (approx.)

The day before serving, place the prunes in a small glass bowl, and pour the wine over them. Refrigerate, covered, overnight.

The next day, transfer the prunes and wine to a small sauce pan, and cook them over low heat for about 30 minutes, or until the prunes are soft.

Drain the prunes, reserving the wine for the sauce, and set them aside.

Cut the pork into ½-inch thick slices, removing any excess fat.

Dredge the slices lightly in the flour, shaking off any excess.

Melt the butter in a large skillet, and sauté the pork slices over medium heat. Do not crowd the pieces together in the skillet.

Brown the pork slowly on both sides; then cook gently until the meat is tender—about 20 minutes.

Season the pork with salt and pepper, and transfer the slices to a shallow baking dish or an ovenproof platter; let the slices overlap slightly.

Arrange a row of prunes on each side of the pork slices.

Cover the platter with foil, and place it in a very slow (200- to 250-degree) oven to keep warm while you make the sauce.

To make the sauce, use the same skillet in which the pork was sautéed.

Add the reserved wine to the skillet, and, with a wire whisk, scrape up any pieces of flour that have stuck to the pan. (This is called *deglazing*.)

Add the jelly, and continue to stir until it is dissolved and blended with the wine.

Cook the sauce for a few minutes over medium-low heat to reduce it slightly.

Bring the sauce to a boil, stirring constantly.

Remove the skillet from the heat, and add ½ cup of the cream.

Return the skillet to the heat, and cook gently until the sauce begins to thicken.

Remove the skillet from the heat again, and add as much of the remaining cream as necessary to make a sauce that will coat a wooden spoon. The more cream you add, the less flavor the sauce will have; however, it should not be too thick.

Pour the sauce over the meat and the prunes, and serve at once.

Serves 4 to 6.

HINT

Fresh pork must be cooked until there is no trace of pink.

CHINESE SPARERIBS

SAUCE:

3 tablespoons honey
3 tablespoons soy sauce
¾ cup packed dark brown sugar
   Pinch of dry mustard
   Dash of Tabasco sauce
2 tablespoons cider vinegar
½ cup catsup
4 garlic cloves, crushed
¼ cup water
2 chicken bouillon cubes

3 pounds of pork spareribs, split

In a medium saucepan, combine all of the sauce ingredients, and cook the mixture over medium heat, stirring, for 5 minutes.

If desired, you can now store this mixture in a jar in the refrigerator for at least one month.

About 1½ hours before serving, parboil the spareribs for 30 minutes in a large kettle with enough water to cover them.

Drain the spareribs well, and place them in a shallow baking pan.

Bake the spareribs at 450 degrees for 15 minutes. Pour off the grease, and reduce the oven heat to 350 degrees.

Brush the spareribs on one side with the sauce, and bake them for 5 minutes.

Turn the ribs, and brush more sauce on the other side; bake another 5 minutes.

Repeat this procedure 3 more times. (In all, each side will be brushed 4 times.)

Serves 4.

Note: Vinegar is used in Chinese cooking to add pungency to a variety of classic dishes.

MARINATED LEG OF LAMB

MARINADE:

⅔ cup olive oil
3 tablespoons lemon juice
  Salt and freshly ground pepper to taste
3 tablespoons chopped parsley
1 teaspoon oregano
3 bay leaves, crumbled
1 cup thinly sliced onions
4 garlic cloves, thinly sliced

1 6- to 7-pound leg of lamb, boned, slit lengthwise (on the
  thin side), laid flat, trimmed of fell and fat
1 teaspoon salt

The day before serving, make the marinade: In a large shallow dish or pan, combine the olive oil, lemon juice, salt, pepper, parsley, oregano, and bay leaves.

Add the onions and garlic.

Lay the meat in the marinade, and spoon some of it over the meat. Cover, and let the meat marinate at room temperature for 12 to 24 hours; turn the meat every few hours.

Preheat the oven to broil, or heat coals on a barbecue grill.

Without drying the meat off, place it, fat side down, on a rack about 4 inches from the heat in the broiler or on a grill rack.

Sprinkle the meat with the salt, and broil for about 15 minutes; do not baste.

Turn the meat with tongs to avoid puncturing it, and moisten it with a little of the marinade; sprinkle it with a little more salt. Broil 12 to 15 minutes longer.

The meat is done when it is pale pink inside with a dark brown crust.

To serve, carve the meat against the grain into thin slices, and place them on a serving platter.

Since this dish is fairly low in calories, it is complemented by any kind of rice, noodle, or potato casserole.

Serves 8 to 10.

HINT

Because of the high acetic acid content of vinegar, it is one of the best (and least expensive) tenderizers for meats. To tenderize any cut of meat quickly, heat 1 cup of beef broth mixed with ½ cup of red wine vinegar, and pour the mixture over the meat. Let the meat marinate for up to 1 hour.

CURRIED LAMB

The fun of serving this dish is setting out several condiments for your guests to place on top as they choose.

---

6 tablespoons unsalted butter
1 5-pound leg of lamb, boned and cut into 1-inch cubes
1 cup finely chopped onion
1 garlic clove, finely chopped
1 apple, cored, peeled, and cut into wedges
¼ cup curry powder (or to taste)
2 tablespoons flour
1 cup peeled, chopped tomatoes, fresh or canned
½ cup raisins
½ cup chicken broth, fresh or canned
1 cup water
   Salt and freshly ground pepper to taste

1 cup heavy cream
1 cup shredded coconut (optional)

Heat the butter in a large kettle or Dutch oven over medium heat, and add the lamb.

Cook the lamb, turning the pieces several times, until no pink shows on the outside.

Add the onion, garlic, and apple wedges; stir. Continue cooking until most of the liquid has evaporated.

Sprinkle the curry powder and flour over the meat mixture, and stir until the meat is well coated.

Add the tomatoes, raisins, chicken broth, water, and salt and pepper to taste; bring to a boil.

Lower the heat, and cook, covered, 1 to 1½ hours, or until the meat is thoroughly tender.

Skim off any fat, and stir in the cream and the optional coconut. Cook just until the cream is heated, but do not allow the sauce to boil.

Taste and correct the seasonings.

Serve the curry with boiled white rice and small bowls of any of the following condiments: chutney, chopped hard-boiled eggs, Spanish peanuts, mashed bananas, raisins, shredded coconut, and chopped onions.

Serves 6 to 8.

COUSCOUS TAGINE

Don't let the lengthy list of ingredients scare you away from trying this savory North African dish. Couscous is imported from France and may be found in gourmet food shops or in Middle Eastern specialty stores. It is a wheat grain, which we call semolina. The ingredients of a tagine (stew) vary seasonally and regionally. Any meat can be used, but lamb and chicken are traditional.

TAGINE:

½ cup olive oil
1½ pounds boneless meat, cut into large chunks
3 cinnamon sticks
10 peppercorns, lightly crushed
1 teaspoon ground cumin
¼ teaspoon saffron
10 whole cloves
¼ teaspoon salt
½ pound dried apricots
½ pound raisins
4 ripe tomatoes, peeled and cut into wedges
2 large onions, cut into wedges
4 carrots, thickly sliced
3 ribs celery, cut into large pieces
1 can (16 ounces) garbanzo beans, drained
1 can (17 ounces) sweet potatoes, drained
2 large zucchini, sliced
6 artichoke hearts, canned
Chicken broth, fresh or canned, to cover
1 box (17 ounces) couscous
Vegetable oil

HARISSA SAUCE:

2 tablespoons cayenne pepper
1 teaspoon fennel seeds
1 teaspoon caraway seeds
1 teaspoon ground cumin
2 garlic cloves, crushed
½ teaspoon salt
1 cup olive oil

FOR GARNISH:

¼ pound dried currants
¼ pound chopped almonds or pine nuts

Heat the oil in a large skillet, and cook the meat until the outside is browned.

Place the meat in a large casserole. Add the spices, apricots, raisins, and tomatoes.

Bake, covered, at 350 degrees for 45 minutes, or until the meat is tender.

Add the vegetables to the casserole, along with enough chicken broth to cover the entire mixture. Bake for another 20 to 30 minutes.

Meanwhile, soak the couscous in cold water for 15 minutes.

Drain, and cook the couscous in a steamer until it is tender— about 10 to 15 minutes.

Remove the couscous from the steamer, and place it on a large platter.

Lightly oil your hands with vegetable oil, and roll the couscous between your palms so that each grain is separated and coated with oil.

Return the couscous to the steamer, and cook it another 10 minutes. Keep it warm.

To prepare the sauce, grind together with a mortar and pestle the spices, garlic, and salt. (This mixture can be prepared at any time and kept in a tightly covered glass jar in the refrigerator until needed.)

A few minutes before serving, add the olive oil to the spice mixture, and place in a small saucepan; cook, stirring constantly, for 5 minutes.

Before serving the tagine, remove the cinnamon sticks and cloves, and discard. Garnish the tagine with the currants and nuts.

Serve the tagine, couscous, and sauce separately. Let your guests mix the three together as they choose.

Serves 6 to 8.

Chicken

The price of chicken certainly isn't what it used to be, but it can still be more economical than most meats. In certain recipes, one 3-pound chicken can serve up to eight people; try doing that with a 3-pound steak or roast!

And chicken has other virtues, too, not the least of which is its versatility. Chicken can be cooked with an incredibly wide variety of ingredients, from wine to fruit to cream sauces; and in each case, you'll end up with a distinctly different main dish.

If a recipe calls for boned chicken breasts, you can realize a slight cost savings by boning them yourself. But you'll need a good boning knife, which is tapered at the end to enable you to get between the meat and the bones. Boning chicken breasts will be easier if they are slightly frozen before you begin.

In all of the following recipes calling for a frying chicken, use one that weighs approximately three pounds. If, of course, your family or guests prefer all dark or all white meat, substitute an equivalent amount of those chicken pieces.

When you buy a frying chicken, chances are you will not be using the liver, giblets, neck, or back in the recipe. Instead of letting these parts go to waste, use them to make a hefty supply of chicken stock. Place the parts in a kettle with water, a tablespoon of salt, some celery leaves, a bay leaf, and a whole peeled onion. Cook the mixture for about an hour. Then strain the broth, and freeze it for use in recipes requiring chicken broth.

CHICKEN DIJON

An easy and flavorful dish when you want something special in a hurry.

　1　frying chicken, cut into serving pieces
¼　cup peanut oil (approx.)
　　Cayenne pepper to taste
½　cup Dijon mustard
　1　cup fine unseasoned bread crumbs
　6　tablespoons melted butter or margarine

Brush the chicken pieces on both sides with the peanut oil, coating them thoroughly.

Sprinkle the chicken with the cayenne pepper to taste.

Place the chicken, skin side up, in a large shallow baking pan, and bake at 350 degrees for 30 minutes.

Remove the chicken from the oven, and turn the heat up to broil.

Brush the skin side of the chicken pieces with the Dijon mustard. (Legs should be brushed on both sides.)

Sprinkle the bread crumbs on the chicken pieces.

Pour the melted butter evenly over the bread crumbs.

Broil the chicken, 6 inches from the heat, for 3 to 5 minutes, or until the coating is golden-brown. Serve.

The broiled chicken can be frozen and reheated, wrapped in foil, in a hot (400-degree) oven.

Serves 4.

BAKED CHICKEN PARMESAN

This is an ideal recipe when you are serving a large number of people because it can easily be doubled or tripled. It can also be assembled in advance and refrigerated or frozen until baking time.

---

2 frying chickens, cut into serving pieces
1½ cups melted butter or margarine
2 to 3 garlic cloves, crushed
2½ tablespoons Dijon mustard
1½ teaspoons Worcestershire sauce
4½ cups fresh unseasoned bread crumbs
1¼ cups freshly grated Parmesan cheese
½ teaspoon salt
⅓ cup chopped parsley

Wash and dry the chicken pieces thoroughly.

In a large shallow dish, combine the melted butter with the garlic, mustard, and Worcestershire sauce.

Combine the bread crumbs with the cheese, salt, and parsley in another dish.

Dip the chicken pieces into the butter mixture; then roll them in the crumb mixture, coating well.

Place the chicken pieces in a large shallow baking dish, and pour the remaining melted butter mixture over them. The dish may be made in advance up to this point.

Bake the chicken at 350 degrees for 1½ hours. Baste with the pan drippings once or twice during the baking time.

Serves 6 to 8.

Reminder: *A clove of garlic is just one of many little pieces that make up a whole garlic bulb. When a recipe calls for a garlic clove, use either a large or a small one, to suit personal tastes.*

CHICKEN CORDON BLEU

With veal prices skyrocketing, why not substitute chicken for the veal in this famous dish? Even if you buy the chicken breasts already boned (sometimes known as "chicken cutlets"), you'll still be saving money compared with the cost of veal cutlets. And what's more important, I think this dish tastes just as good!

---

  6 whole chicken breasts, skinned and boned
     Salt and freshly ground pepper to taste
  6 thin slices prosciutto or baked ham
  6 thin slices Gruyère or Swiss cheese
  2 eggs, lightly beaten
  1 teaspoon water
  1 cup flour
1½ cups fresh unseasoned bread crumbs
  ½ cup butter
     Parsley sprigs for garnish (optional)

Open up each chicken breast, keeping the two halves intact, and season with salt and pepper to taste.

On one side of each breast, place a slice each of ham and cheese. Fold the breast back in half.

Beat the eggs with the water in a shallow bowl.

Carefully dredge the chicken breasts in the flour; then dip them in the egg mixture, and finally in the bread crumbs until well coated.

Place the breasts on a wire rack, and refrigerate for 2 hours. (This enables the bread crumbs to adhere better while the breasts are being cooked.)

About 30 minutes before serving, melt the butter in a large skillet.

When it is hot but not smoking, sauté the chicken breasts until golden-brown on all sides. This will take 20 to 30 minutes.

To serve the breasts, arrange them on a heated serving platter. Garnish them with parsley sprigs, if desired.

If not serving the chicken right away, place it in a large shallow baking pan, cover with foil, and keep warm in a slow (200-degree) oven.

Serves 6.

HINT

You will have a ready supply of bread crumbs if you save the heels from all your bread, plus any additional stale bread. Place the bread in a plastic bag and freeze it until needed; you can make crumbs by placing the slices directly from the freezer into a blender or a food processor. You can also make bread crumbs first and then freeze them for use in any recipe.

CHICKEN ENCHILADAS

2 whole chicken breasts
1 teaspoon salt
2 tablespoons butter or margarine
1 medium onion, chopped
1 garlic clove, crushed
1 can (3 ounces) chopped chilis, well drained
1 can (16 ounces) tomatoes with the liquid
1 can (8 ounces) tomato sauce
1 teaspoon sugar
1 teaspoon ground cumin
½ teaspoon salt
½ teaspoon oregano
½ teaspoon basil

12 frozen corn tortillas
2 cups grated Monterey Jack cheese
¾ cup sour cream

Place the chicken breasts in a large saucepan with enough water to cover them and add the teaspoon of salt. Cook, covered, over medium heat until the chicken is tender—about 20 minutes. Remove from the heat.

Meanwhile, prepare a tomato sauce: In a medium saucepan, melt the butter, and sauté the onion and garlic until the onion is golden.

Add the chilis, tomatoes, tomato sauce, sugar, and seasonings; simmer, covered, for 20 minutes. Remove from the heat.

When the chicken is cool enough to handle, remove the skin and bones, and discard; cut the meat into 12 strips.

Separate the tortillas while they're still frozen. Using a pair of tongs, dip each one into the tomato sauce for about 10 seconds to soften it.

Place one piece of chicken and about 2 tablespoons of the grated cheese in the middle of each tortilla. Roll it in thirds, and place it, seam side down, in a greased 9 × 13 × 2-inch baking pan.

Combine the sour cream with the remaining tomato sauce, and pour it over the tortillas. Be sure to cover them completely with the sauce, or they will dry out while baking.

Sprinkle the remaining cheese on top. The dish may be assembled in advance to this point and refrigerated or frozen.

Bake, covered with foil, at 350 degrees for 40 minutes. If baking directly from the freezer, increase the baking time to 1 hour.

Serves 4 to 6.

HINT

To keep sour cream longer, store it upside-down in the refrigerator so that air cannot enter the container.

●

CHICKEN FIESTA CASSEROLE

This is the way Mexican cooks use up leftover or stale tortillas. You can use frozen and thawed tortillas, or the refrigerated variety.

¼ cup vegetable oil
18 6-inch corn tortillas, cut into ½-inch strips
1 large onion, finely chopped
4 medium tomatoes, peeled, seeded, and chopped
2 tablespoons chili powder
   Salt and freshly ground pepper to taste
1 teaspoon sugar
1½ cups heavy cream
4 to 6 cups cooked, shredded chicken (preferably all white meat)
1½ cups grated Monterey Jack cheese

In a large skillet, heat the oil over medium-high heat and fry the tortilla strips, turning once; do not brown. Drain the strips well on paper towels.

Pour off all but 2 tablespoons of the oil, and sauté the onion over medium heat for 3 minutes, stirring constantly.

Add the tomatoes, chili powder, salt and pepper to taste, and sugar. Simmer gently until the sauce is well blended.

Grease a large casserole or baking dish. Pour in enough sauce to coat the bottom lightly.

Place one-fourth of the tortilla strips over the sauce.

Pour one-fourth of the cream over the strips, and top with one-third of the chicken and one-third of the sauce.

Repeat twice, ending with the remaining quarter of tortilla strips and cream.

Sprinkle the cheese over the top.

The dish may be made in advance and refrigerated or frozen at this point.

Bake, uncovered, at 350 degrees for 30 minutes, or until the cheese has melted and the dish is thoroughly heated. If baking directly from the freezer, increase the baking time to 1 hour.

Serves 6.

Note: If there is not enough sauce, you can stretch it by adding ½ cup of fresh or canned chicken broth and 4 to 6 tablespoons of tomato paste.

YUCATAN CHICKEN

This is an Americanized version of a popular Mexican dish.

---

6 to 8 whole chicken breasts, cut in half
2 tablespoons chili powder (approx.)
2 tablespoons curry powder (approx.)
1 large onion, finely chopped
3 medium tomatoes, peeled and chopped
3 stalks celery, chopped
1 green pepper, chopped
4 cups orange juice

Line a large shallow baking pan with aluminum foil.

Season the chicken thickly with the chili and curry.

Place the chicken in the prepared pan, and distribute the onion, tomatoes, celery, and green pepper over the chicken pieces.

Pour the orange juice over everything, and marinate the chicken in the refrigerator for several hours.

Cover the pan with foil, and bake at 300 degrees for 4 hours. Slow cooking is most important to achieve the correct flavor and consistency.

Serve with boiled white rice, or with fried, buttered tortillas.

Serves 6 to 8.

CHICKEN KIEV

A classic chicken dish that is not as hard to fix as you may think because the whole thing can be made in advance.

HERB BUTTER:

¾ cup butter, softened
  Pinch of salt
  Freshly ground pepper to taste
  Pinch of rosemary
½ teaspoon garlic powder
1 tablespoon chopped parsley
1 teaspoon dried tarragon

CHICKEN:

6 whole chicken breasts, boned, skinned, and cut in half
1 cup flour
3 eggs, well beaten
1 cup dry unseasoned bread crumbs
  Oil or shortening for deep-frying

One or more days before serving, make the herb butter: In a small bowl, cream the butter with the seasonings and herbs.

Place the butter mixture on a sheet of waxed paper, and cover with another sheet of waxed paper. Press flat.

Wrap the butter well, and freeze for several hours, or until firm, before using.

Place each chicken breast half between two sheets of waxed paper, and pound with a mallet or a knife handle until it is about ¼-inch thick. Try not to break up the meat.

Remove the herb butter from the freezer, and cut it into 24 small pieces.

Place 2 pieces of butter in the middle of each breast half; bring the sides of the meat together, fold the ends into the middle, and secure with toothpicks. Make sure that no butter shows.

Roll the breasts in the flour.

Dip them in the beaten eggs, and roll them in the bread crumbs.

When all the pieces are coated, refrigerate them, covered, until well chilled—about 1 hour.

In a heavy skillet, heat about 2 inches of oil to 375 degrees. Use a deep-fat thermometer to gauge heat.

Add the chicken, and fry until golden-brown on all sides. Use a pair of tongs to turn the chicken, to avoid piercing the meat.

Drain the chicken well on paper towels. Serve immediately, or let the chicken cool thoroughly; wrap the pieces individually, and freeze them until needed.

To reheat, unwrap the desired number of servings, and bake them, uncovered, in a shallow baking pan at 350 degrees for 35 to 40 minutes or until well heated. Remove the toothpicks before serving.

Serves 6.

HINT

Fats should be stored in a dark, dry, cool place.

CHINESE WALNUT CHICKEN

This low-calorie, low-cholesterol dish must be cooked in a wok.

---

2 whole chicken breasts, skinned and boned
2 tablespoons cornstarch
2 tablespoons dry cocktail sherry
3 tablespoons soy sauce
  Peanut oil
1 onion, finely chopped
3 stalks celery, sliced on the diagonal
1 can (8½ ounces) bamboo shoots, well drained
1 can (8½ ounces) water chestnuts, well drained and sliced
1 cup coarsely chopped walnuts
2 cups fresh bean sprouts *or* 1 can (16 ounces) bean sprouts,
  well drained
1 pound mushrooms, wiped clean and sliced
⅓ cup fresh or canned chicken broth
  Salt and freshly ground pepper to taste

Several hours before serving, cut the chicken into bite-sized pieces.

In a small bowl, combine the cornstarch, sherry, and soy sauce, beating with a wire whisk until smooth.

Place the chicken in this mixture, stirring well, and refrigerate for at least 2 hours.

Set out all the vegetables near the stove.

Heat 2 tablespoons of oil in a wok over medium heat. When the oil starts to sizzle, add the onion and celery. Stir-fry continuously, until the vegetables are bright and translucent but still crisp. Push the cooked vegetables up the sides of the wok.

Add 2 more tablespoons of oil, if necessary, and when hot, add the bamboo shoots and water chestnuts; cook in the same manner for 2 minutes. Push these vegetables up the sides of the wok.

Add 2 more tablespoons of oil, if needed, and add the walnuts, bean sprouts, and mushrooms; proceed as above. (Mushrooms should stay firm and fairly light in color.)

Add 2 more tablespoons of oil, and, when hot, sauté the chicken pieces for 3 to 5 minutes, stirring constantly. To test the chicken for doneness, remove a piece and slice in half. The meat should be white.

The entire recipe can be made in advance up to this point. If not serving right away, turn off the heat, remove any excess oil, and cover the wok. It is not necessary to refrigerate the dish, but do not leave it standing for more than 2 hours.

To complete the recipe, or to reheat it: Using a wooden spoon, make a well in the center of all the food.

Over medium heat, pour the chicken broth into the well. When the broth begins to boil, stir everything together. (The steam from the broth will reheat the food without allowing the vegetables to get soggy.)

Season with salt and pepper to taste, and serve immediately with boiled white rice or Chinese Oven Rice. (See recipe on page 137.) You can also serve miniature egg rolls (available in the freezer department at most supermarkets) with this dish.

Serves 4 to 6.

ITALIAN-STYLE STUFFED CHICKEN

1 cup ricotta cheese
1 egg
½ cup freshly grated Parmesan cheese
½ teaspoon garlic salt
2 packages (10 ounces each) frozen chopped spinach, thawed and well drained
1 3½-pound roasting chicken
2 tablespoons olive oil
1 tablespoon melted butter or margarine

¼ teaspoon rosemary
½ teaspoon oregano
½ teaspoon dried thyme

In a small bowl, combine the ricotta, egg, Parmesan cheese, and garlic salt; stir in the drained chopped spinach.

With a sharp knife, cut the chicken completely down the front, splitting the breast bone.

Press the chicken down to "pop" the bones, so that it will lie flat.

Gently, using your fingers and/or a boning knife, loosen the skin from the breast portions. Try not to tear the skin. (Do not loosen the skin covering the wings or the legs.)

Place the chicken, skin side up, in a shallow baking pan.

Place the ricotta-spinach mixture in the areas between the skin and the breast of the chicken.

Press down with your hands to distribute the stuffing evenly.

Combine the oil, butter, rosemary, oregano, and thyme, and brush this mixture over the entire chicken.

Bake the chicken at 350 degrees for about 1½ hours, brushing occasionally with the pan juices.

If the parts of the stretched skin begin to burn, cover them with pieces of foil.

To serve, cut the chicken into quarters. Serve with your favorite variety of pasta, tossed with butter and a little garlic salt, and a tossed green salad.

Serves 4.

COQ AU VIN

A simple chicken dish that never goes out of style. Serve it with boiled, parslied new potatoes and crusty French bread.

---

 2 tablespoons vegetable oil
 8 tablespoons butter
 1 frying chicken, cut into serving pieces
 1 pound small whole mushrooms, wiped clean
 1 can (16 ounces) small white onions, drained
½ teaspoon salt
¼ cup cognac or brandy
 3 cups dry red wine
 1 to 1½ cups fresh or canned beef bouillon
 1 tablespoon tomato paste
 2 garlic cloves, finely chopped
    Pinch of dried thyme
 1 bay leaf
 3 tablespoons flour
    Chopped parsley for garnish (optional)

In a large kettle or Dutch oven, heat the oil with 6 tablespoons of the butter.

Cook the chicken pieces over medium-high heat until golden-brown on all sides.

Add the mushrooms, onions, and salt, and cook the mixture, covered, over medium heat for 10 minutes, turning the chicken once.

Gently warm the cognac in a small butter melter; uncover the chicken, and add the cognac.

Carefully ignite the mixture with a wooden kitchen match, and shake the kettle back and forth until the flame dies out.

Add the wine, and just enough beef bouillon to cover the chicken.

Stir in the tomato paste, garlic, thyme, and bay leaf.

Bring to a boil; reduce the heat and simmer, covered, for 25 to 30 minutes.

When the chicken is done, remove the pieces and keep them warm.

Skim off any fat from the cooking liquid.

Bring the liquid to a boil, and cook over medium-high heat until it is reduced to about 2½ cups. Taste, and adjust the seasonings.

Remove the kettle from the heat; remove and discard the bay leaf.

In a small bowl, combine the flour with the remaining 2 tablespoons of butter to form a smooth paste.

Using a wire whisk, stir this mixture into the hot cooking liquid, and bring the sauce to a simmer.

Cook the sauce, stirring, for a few minutes, or until the sauce is thick enough to coat a wooden spoon.

Add the chicken to the kettle, and reheat it for about 2 minutes.

To serve, transfer the chicken and sauce to a casserole or serving bowl; garnish with chopped parsley, if desired.

This dish can be made ahead and refrigerated or frozen until needed. Reheat it in a covered casserole at 300 degrees for 1 hour.

Serves 4.

HINT

To ignite any alcohol (brandy, rum, etc.), you must gently heat it first, to allow the alcohol vapors to rise. If, however, you boil the liquid, the alcohol will evaporate completely, and it will never ignite.

PIQUANT CHICKEN BREASTS

A truly unique chicken dish that is child's play to prepare. Because there is a lot of cooking liquid, serve this dish over white rice; you won't want to waste any of the tasty sauce!

1½ cups rosé or dry red wine
 ½ cup soy sauce
 ½ cup salad oil
  2 garlic cloves, sliced
 ½ cup water
  2 teaspoons powdered ginger
 ½ teaspoon oregano
  2 tablespoons brown sugar
  4 whole chicken breasts, cut in half

In a large bowl, combine all of the ingredients except the chicken; mix well.

Place the chicken breasts in a large casserole or baking dish, and pour the sauce on top.

Bake, uncovered, at 375 degrees for 1 hour, or until the chicken is fork-tender.

Serve over boiled white rice.

Serves 4.

CHICKEN PUFFS

4 to 6 chicken breasts, halved, skinned, and boned
½ lemon
1½ cups pancake mix
1 cup milk
1 egg
⅛ teaspoon cayenne pepper
Oil for deep-frying

Rub the chicken with the fresh lemon.

Cut the chicken into small pieces, about 1 × 1 inch.

In a medium bowl combine the pancake mix, milk, egg, and cayenne, mixing until smooth; there should be no lumps.

In a deep-fat fryer or large skillet heat about 2 inches of oil to 375 degrees. If your fryer is not equipped with a thermometer, use a deep-fat thermometer.

Dip the chicken pieces into the batter, using a slotted spoon. (If the batter seems too thick, add a little more milk.)

Fry the chicken until it is puffed and golden-brown—about 1 to 2 minutes.

Drain the chicken on paper towels and serve hot with boiled white rice as a main dish; or as an appetizer, spear the pieces with toothpicks, and serve them with honey, tartar sauce, or cocktail sauce.

Serves 4 to 6.

Note: You can substitute 1½ pounds of peeled raw shrimp for the chicken.

POLYNESIAN CHICKEN

One of my favorite make-ahead main dishes for a large crowd.

---

3 frying chickens, cut into serving pieces
3 cans (16 ounces each) fruits for salad
¾ cup soy sauce
1 garlic clove, finely crushed
3 jars (10 ounces each) prepared sweet and sour sauce

The day before serving, wash and dry the chicken pieces. Arrange them, skin side up, in a large shallow baking pan.

Drain the fruit, reserving the syrup. Cover the fruit, and refrigerate.

Pour the reserved syrup and the soy sauce evenly over the chicken. Add the garlic.

Bake, uncovered, at 350 degrees for 1 hour, or until the chicken is a rich golden-brown. Turn the chicken often so that all pieces brown evenly.

Pour the liquid from the baking pan into a large saucepan.

Leave the chicken in the pan, cover tightly with foil, and set aside.

Add the sweet and sour sauce to the liquid in the pan; bring to a boil over medium heat.

Continue simmering until the sauce thickens and is reduced to about 3½ cups—about 45 minutes.

Pour the sauce over the chicken, and refrigerate, covered, overnight.

About 1 hour before serving, bake the chicken and sauce, uncovered, at 350 degrees for 30 minutes.

Add the reserved fruit, and continue baking for 20 minutes, basting often.

Serve hot, with boiled white rice or Chinese Oven Rice. (See recipe on page 137.)

Serves 10 to 12.

CHICKEN MARENGO

This dish was reputedly composed on the spot by Napoleon's chef to commemorate his victory at the Battle of Marengo.

1 frying chicken, cut into serving pieces
2 tablespoons olive oil (approx.)
1 garlic clove
2 medium onions, finely chopped
3 tomatoes, peeled and chopped
1 pound small whole mushrooms, wiped clean
1 can (6 ounces) tomato paste
⅔ cup dry white wine
  Salt and freshly ground pepper to taste
  Pinch of parsley
  Pinch of dried thyme

Wash and dry the chicken pieces.

In a large kettle or Dutch oven, heat the oil over medium-high heat.

Add the garlic clove, and cook until it turns brown; remove and discard.

Add the chicken pieces to the hot oil, and sauté until golden-brown on all sides.

Add more oil if necessary, and, when hot, add the onions, tomatoes, mushrooms, tomato paste, wine, and seasonings.

Bring to a boil; reduce the heat and simmer, covered, for about 1 hour or until the chicken is tender.

Serve hot, with buttered egg or spinach noodles, French bread, and white wine.

Serves 4.

HINT

Dry vermouth can be used in almost any recipe calling for dry white wine. It is cheaper than wine, it keeps longer, and it is delicately flavored with herbs.

SURE SUCCESS MOIST TURKEY

This recipe is for people who are tired of dry, tasteless turkey.

PASTE:

 2 tablespoons salt
 2 tablespoons garlic salt
 ¾ tablespoon poultry seasoning
 1 tablespoon pepper
 ¼ cup paprika

 1 20-pound turkey, rinsed with water and wiped dry

STUFFING:

 1 cup butter or margarine
 2 cups chopped onion
 2 to 3 cups chopped celery
 1½ pounds Ritz crackers, finely crushed
 2 pounds mushrooms, wiped clean and sliced
 2 eggs
 ½ teaspoon salt
 1 carrot, sliced into strips

BASTING MIXTURE:

 1 cup Sauterne (or other white wine)
 1 cup water
 ½ cup melted butter or margarine

The day before serving, make a paste by combining all the spices with enough warm water to make a thick mixture.

Rub this paste all over the turkey, inside and out.

Cover the turkey loosely with foil, and refrigerate overnight.

The next day, make the stuffing. Melt ½ cup of the butter in a large skillet, and sauté the onions and celery until tender— about 5 minutes.

Place the crushed crackers in a large bowl, and add the sautéed onions and celery, plus any butter remaining in the skillet.

Melt the remaining ½ cup of butter in the skillet, and sauté the mushrooms until soft—about 10 minutes.

Add the sautéed mushrooms to the cracker mixture, along with the eggs, salt, and carrot; mix well.

Use this mixture to stuff the chest and neck cavities of the turkey, packing it loosely. Place the stuffed turkey in a large roasting pan.

To make the basting liquid, combine the wine, water, and melted butter, and pour over the turkey.

Place the pan in the oven, and bake the turkey at 325 degrees for about 7 hours, or until the juices run clear when the thigh is pricked with a fork.

Baste the turkey frequently with the liquids in the roasting pan.

If the breast portion seems to be browning too quickly, cover it with foil.

Serves 15 to 20.

PAELLA

For a really adventurous cook.

---

1 frying chicken, cut into serving pieces
  Salt
½ cup olive oil (approx.)
2 medium onions, finely chopped
1 garlic clove, finely chopped
2 or 3 rock lobster tails, cut into 1-inch pieces
½ pound shrimp, shelled and deveined
1 thick ham slice, diced
½ pound Spanish sausage (or pepperoni), sliced
2 to 3 ripe tomatoes, peeled and chopped
  1 bay leaf
3 cups long-grain raw rice
  Pinch of saffron
6 cups boiling water
1 dozen clams in the shell, scrubbed (optional)
½ cup canned peas or green beans (optional)
  Black and green pitted olives for garnish
1 lemon, cut in 8 wedges for garnish

Wash and dry the chicken pieces, and season them with salt.

Heat ¼ cup of the olive oil in a large skillet, and sauté the chicken with the onions and garlic until it is golden-brown.

Add the lobster and shrimp; sauté a few minutes, adding more oil if needed.

Remove the mixture from the skillet, and keep warm.

In the same skillet, combine the ham, sausage, tomatoes and bay leaf.

Add the rice and saffron; pour the boiling water over all, and bring to a boil, stirring constantly. Remove the skillet from the heat.

Pour the rice mixture into a paella pan or any large baking

pan. Arrange the chicken mixture on top of the rice; add the optional clams and peas or green beans.

Place the pan on the floor of the oven and bake, uncovered, at 325 degrees for 25 to 30 minutes, or until all the liquid is absorbed and the rice is tender. Do not stir after the pan goes into the oven.

To serve, remove the bay leaf and discard. Garnish the paella with the olives and lemon wedges. Serve with a salad made of romaine lettuce, thinly sliced red onions, and mandarin oranges; use an olive oil dressing to complement the flavor of the paella.

Serves 4 to 6.

HINT

Fresh tomatoes keep longer if stored with the stems down.

JAMBALAYA

Sensational and versatile. Add or subtract ingredients to suit personal tastes.

---

  3 frying chickens, cut into serving pieces
½ cup butter or margarine (approx.)
  6 tablespoons vegetable oil
¾ pound cooked ham, diced
  1 green pepper, coarsely chopped
  1 large onion, finely chopped
  2 ribs celery, cut in large chunks
  4 tomatoes, peeled, seeded, and chopped
½ teaspoon salt
  1 bay leaf
  2 garlic cloves, finely chopped
     Dash of Tabasco sauce
½ teaspoon dried crushed red pepper
  2 cups water
  1 package (10 ounces) frozen corn, thawed (optional)
1½ cups long-grain raw rice
  1 pound cooked shrimp, shelled and deveined

Wash and dry the chicken pieces. In a large kettle or Dutch oven, heat the butter and oil over medium-high heat.

Brown the chicken pieces, a few at a time, until golden-brown on all sides.

Remove the pieces as they brown, and place them in a large shallow baking dish; bake at 325 degrees for 30 minutes.

Meanwhile, add more butter to the kettle if necessary, and sauté the ham, green pepper, onion, and celery for about 5 minutes.

Add the tomatoes, seasonings, water, and optional corn to the kettle, and bring the mixture to a boil.

Stir in the rice; cover, and simmer over medium-low heat for 20 minutes, or until all the liquid is absorbed.

Add the shrimp and the baked chicken during the last 5 minutes of cooking time.

Let the jambalaya stand, covered, for 10 minutes, or until all the liquid is absorbed.

Remove the bay leaf and discard. Taste for seasoning.

Serves 8 to 10.

Fish and Seafood

SHRIMP CREOLE

---

2 tablespoons butter or margarine
1 tablespoon flour
1 cup finely chopped onion
1 cup finely chopped celery
1 can (28 ounces) tomatoes
1 green pepper, seeded and diced
½ teaspoon dried thyme
2 teaspoons chopped parsley
2 bay leaves
½ teaspoon garlic powder
1 tablespoon paprika
¼ teaspoon cayenne pepper
1 teaspoon salt
1½ pounds shrimp, shelled and deveined
2 tablespoons cornstarch
¼ cup water

In a large skillet, melt the butter, and add the flour, stirring constantly; cook until golden-brown.

Add the onion and celery, and cook, stirring constantly, for 3 minutes.

Drain the tomatoes, reserving one cup of liquid. Add the tomatoes and the reserved liquid to the skillet, along with the green pepper, spices, and salt.

Cover the pan, and simmer for 20 minutes, stirring occasionally.

Add the shrimp; bring the mixture to a boil, and cook about 3 minutes, or until the shrimp are pink and firm. Do not overcook them.

Combine the cornstarch with the water in a small bowl, mixing well.

Stir this mixture into the skillet, and cook over low heat for another 2 to 3 minutes.

Remove the bay leaves and discard.

Serve the shrimp creole over boiled white rice.

Serves 6.

MEXICAN SHRIMP

Hot, delicious, and simple.

---

2 tablespoons olive oil
2 garlic cloves, crushed
2 tablespoons flour
2 tablespoons prepared chili sauce
2 teaspoons chili powder
2 cups milk
¼ cup dry cocktail sherry
¼ cup finely chopped parsley
1½ pounds shrimp, shelled and deveined

In a large skillet, heat the oil, and brown the garlic.

Add the flour, chili sauce, chili powder, and milk, stirring constantly.

Cook slowly, continuing to stir, until the sauce thickens.

Add the sherry, parsley, and shrimp.

Pour the mixture into a casserole, and bake at 325 degrees for 30 minutes.

Serve over boiled white rice.

Serves 4.

HINT

For cooking purposes dry cocktail sherry, which is pale whitish yellow in color, is the best. Medium sherry can also be used although its nutty flavor tends to overpower that of other ingredients. Do not, however, use cream sherry unless it is specifically called for (usually in dessert recipes).

COQUILLES ST. JACQUES AU GRATIN

After tasting this dish, you'll never order it at a restaurant again. It can be made ahead and set aside until the final reheating.

SCALLOPS:

1½ pounds bay or sea scallops
  1 cup dry white wine
  ¼ cup water
  ¼ cup unsalted butter
  3 large shallots, finely chopped
  1 pound mushrooms, wiped clean and thinly sliced
  ¼ cup finely chopped parsley

SAUCE:

  2 tablespoons butter
2½ tablespoons flour
  1 cup reserved cooking liquid from scallops (approx.)
  ½ cup dry white wine
  ½ cup heavy cream
     Salt and freshly ground pepper to taste
  1 egg yolk

TOPPING:

  ½ cup unseasoned bread crumbs
  1 cup finely grated Swiss cheese
  2 tablespoons butter

Wash the scallops well to remove grit and sand; drain thoroughly on paper towels.

In a saucepan, combine the wine with the water, and bring to a boil.

Add the scallops, and simmer, stirring once or twice, for 3 to 5 minutes. Do not overcook.

Remove the scallops with a slotted spoon, and set them aside. Reserve the cooking liquid for the sauce.

Melt the butter in a skillet, and add the shallots and mushrooms. Cook, stirring, for 5 minutes.

Add the parsley; stir, and remove from the heat.

Thinly slice the scallops crosswise, and add them to the mushrooms. Set aside.

To make the sauce, melt the butter in a saucepan over low heat.

With a wire whisk, stir in the flour. Cook this *roux*, stirring constantly, for 3 minutes.

Remove from the heat and let cool for a minute. Add about 1 cup of the reserved cooking liquid and an additional ½ cup of wine.

Return the mixture to the heat, and bring to a boil; reduce the heat, and simmer the sauce, stirring constantly, for a few minutes.

Stir in the cream, and simmer 2 minutes longer. Add salt and pepper to taste.

Check the sauce for consistency. It should not be too thick. If it is, add a little more reserved cooking liquid. If it is too thin, simply simmer it a bit longer.

Remove the sauce from the heat, and let it cool.

Add a few spoonfuls of the sauce to the egg yolk, and return this mixture to the sauce, stirring well to blend.

Pour the sauce over the scallop mixture, and mix together lightly.

Transfer the mixture to a buttered shallow baking dish or into individual baking dishes or scallop shells.

Sprinkle the top with the bread crumbs and cheese; dot with the remaining butter. Set aside until needed, or refrigerate for several hours or overnight. Do not freeze.

Bake at 425 degrees for 10 to 15 minutes, or until the top is nicely browned and the mixture is thoroughly heated.

Serve immediately with white wine, French bread, and/or boiled white rice. A simple salad will set off this rich dish nicely.

Serves 4 to 6. (Will also serve 8 as an appetizer.)

CRAB MEAT AND ARTICHOKE CASSEROLE

1 can (20 ounces) whole artichoke hearts, drained
1 pound fresh crab meat, with shell and cartilage removed
4 tablespoons butter
¾ pound mushrooms, wiped clean and sliced
2½ tablespoons flour
1 cup heavy cream
  Salt and freshly ground pepper to taste
  Pinch of cayenne pepper
1 tablespoon Worcestershire sauce
¼ cup dry cocktail sherry
⅓ cup grated Parmesan cheese

Arrange the artichoke hearts in a buttered shallow baking dish; spread the crab meat over them.

In a medium skillet, melt 2 tablespoons of the butter, and sauté the mushrooms for 5 minutes. Then spread them over the crab meat.

Over low heat, make a *roux* by melting the remaining 2 tablespoons of butter in a saucepan and stirring in the flour. Stir constantly for 2 minutes with a wire whisk; do not let the mixture brown.

Gradually add the cream, stirring until the sauce is smooth.

Add the salt and pepper to taste, cayenne, Worcestershire sauce, and sherry. Pour the sauce over the casserole, and sprinkle the grated cheese on top.

The dish can be assembled in advance up to this point and refrigerated.

Bake at 375 degrees for 20 minutes, or until sauce is bubbly.

Serves 4.

DEVILED LOBSTER TAILS

This dish is quite elegant, yet it's very simple to prepare.

---

2 pounds lobster tails
¼ cup butter
2 stalks celery, chopped
1 green pepper, seeded and finely chopped
1 medium onion, finely chopped
1 garlic clove, finely chopped
   Pinch of salt
   Freshly ground pepper to taste
1 cup bread crumbs (Italian-style or unseasoned)
   Pinch of cayenne pepper
   Pinch of dry mustard
   Dash of Worcestershire sauce
⅛ teaspoon lemon juice
   Additional butter for topping

If using fresh lobster tails, drop them into boiling water and cook for 10 to 13 minutes. If using frozen tails, follow package directions for cooking.

When cooked, remove the tails from the water and drain.

With kitchen shears, cut away the membrane covering the tail, and lift out the meat. (Try to keep the shells intact if you plan to serve the meat in them.) Cut the meat into bite-sized pieces, and set aside.

In a large skillet, melt the butter, and add the celery, green pepper, onion, and garlic. Cook over low heat until tender, about 5 minutes.

Season the mixture with salt and pepper, and add the bread crumbs, blending well.

Add the lobster meat, cayenne, dry mustard, Worcestershire sauce, and lemon juice, mixing well.

Fill the lobster shells with this mixture. You can also use a buttered shallow baking dish or individual scallop shells.

Dot the tops with additional butter. (If you wish, you can also sprinkle on a little Parmesan cheese.)

The dish can be assembled in advance up to this point and refrigerated.

Bake at 400 degrees for 15 to 20 minutes, or until top is lightly browned.

Serves 4.

LAZY COOK'S BOUILLABAISSE

Bouillabaisse is an aromatic fish stew that is a specialty of the French port city of Marseilles. A real bouillabaisse is a work of art, but this quick version is quite simple to fix. It's low in cholesterol, too.

¼ cup margarine or vegetable oil
1 large onion, finely chopped
1 cup chopped celery
2 cans (28 ounces each) concentrated crushed tomatoes
2 pounds boneless fish fillets (haddock, perch, cod, or a mixture), cut into large chunks
1 teaspoon basil
1 teaspoon Worcestershire sauce
  Pinch of salt
1 can (6½ ounces) tuna, packed in water
1 can (6½ ounces) minced clams

In a large kettle or Dutch oven, heat the margarine or oil.

Add the onion and celery, and cook over medium heat until the vegetables are soft but not brown.

Add the tomatoes, fish, basil, Worcestershire sauce, and salt.

Reduce the heat and cook, covered, for 45 minutes, or until the fish is thoroughly cooked.

During the last 5 minutes of cooking, drain the tuna, and add it to the kettle. Add the clams, along with some of the liquid.

Serve the stew in bowls, accompanied with your favorite bread and salad.

The stew can also be refrigerated for several days and gently reheated.

Serves 4 to 6.

FRENCH SOLE

This belongs to the "best I've ever eaten" category. Sole is normally bland, but it comes to life when combined with other ingredients. Great care should be taken not to overcook it.

---

   4 large sole fillets (about 2 pounds)
1½ pounds mushrooms, wiped clean and sliced
     Juice of ½ lemon
 ⅓ cup chopped parsley
 ¼ cup melted butter
     Salt and freshly ground pepper to taste
     Pinch of nutmeg
   1 cup finely ground blanched almonds
 ½ to 1 cup dry white wine

Lightly score the sole fillets by making parallel, diagonal lines with a knife on the skin side to prevent them from contracting while cooking.

Place the sliced mushrooms, lemon juice, parsley, melted butter, salt and pepper to taste, and nutmeg in a large bowl.

Force the ground almonds through a sieve to remove the lumps, and add them to the mushrooms, mixing well. (If the mixture is too dry, add a little more melted butter.)

Butter a large shallow baking dish, and spread the mushroom mixture over the bottom.

Lay the sole fillets on top of the mushroom mixture, arranging them close together, but do not overlap them. Sprinkle with additional salt and pepper.

Lift up the fillets at the corners, and pour in the wine.

The dish is now ready to cook, but it may be prepared ahead to this point and refrigerated. To store, cover the dish with buttered waxed paper, placing the buttered side directly on top of the fish. If chilled, the dish must come to room temperature before it is baked.

Bake the fish, uncovered, on the middle rack of a 500-degree oven for 10 to 12 minutes, or until the fish flakes when lightly poked with a fork.

This fish will go well with any kind of potatoes or rice. Serve the same kind of wine as you use in the recipe.

Serves 4 to 6.

BAKED SOLE

¼ teaspoon salt
⅛ teaspoon freshly ground pepper
⅛ teaspoon ground mace
⅛ teaspoon dried thyme
2 pounds sole fillets
¼ cup dry vermouth
2½ tablespoons lemon juice
3 tablespoons melted butter
3 tablespoons butter for sautéing
½ pound mushrooms, wiped clean and sliced
¼ cup finely chopped onion
Lemon wedges and chopped parsley for garnish

In a small bowl, combine the salt, pepper, mace, and thyme.

Dust both sides of the fillets with this mixture, and place the fillets in a lightly greased baking dish.

Combine the vermouth, lemon juice, and melted butter, and pour this over the fish.

Melt the remaining butter in a skillet, and sauté the mushrooms until tender.

Add the onion, and cook another 2 minutes.

Spoon the onion-mushroom mixture evenly over the fillets.

Bake at 350 degrees for 20 minutes, or until the fish is opaque and flakes when lightly poked with a fork.

Serve the fish garnished with lemon wedges and chopped parsley.

Serves 4.

Meatless

HOMEMADE PASTA

A good basic recipe for all kinds of pasta.

1½ cups all-purpose flour
 1 egg
 1 egg white
 1 tablespoon olive oil
   Pinch of salt
   Water as needed

Place the flour in a large bowl and make a well in the center. Pour the egg, egg white, oil, and salt into the well.

Using your fingers or a fork, mix the liquid ingredients into the flour until the dough is consistent. Gather the dough into a rough ball.

Gradually add enough water to hold the ball together, working it into the dough.

Knead the dough on a lightly floured surface until it is smooth, shiny, and elastic, approximately 5-10 minutes. (A pastry blender or food processor can be used.)

Wrap the ball in waxed paper, and let it dry for about 15 minutes.

If you have a pasta machine, take small amounts of dough at a time and let the machine cut the noodles; allow them to dry well before cooking them.

If you are going to cut the noodles by hand, roll the dough on a lightly floured surface in many directions; flour the dough only enough to prevent it from sticking.

Cut the dough into 4-inch squares.

Working with one square at a time, fold it in half, and cut

into strips of desired width; open the noodles out on a clean cloth to dry slightly before cooking.

Cook the noodles in 6 quarts of rapidly boiling salted water for 7 to 10 minutes or until they are just *al dente* (tender).

Makes about ¾ pound of noodles.

RAVIOLI WITH SPINACH FILLING

FILLING:

  1 cup grated Parmesan cheese
1½ cups ricotta cheese
  1 egg yolk
  1 package (10 ounces) frozen chopped spinach, thawed and
     well drained
 ¼ teaspoon nutmeg
   Garlic salt to taste
   Freshly ground pepper to taste

   Homemade pasta (use preceding pasta recipe)

Combine all the ingredients for the filling; taste, and correct the seasoning.

Prepare the pasta as directed in the preceding recipe on page 118, and roll it out very thinly.

Keep any pasta you are not working with covered with a damp cloth to prevent it from drying out.

Cut a strip approximately 8 inches long by 4 inches wide, using the edge of a towel to form a straight border.

Place small amounts of the filling on the pasta, spacing each mound of filling about 1½ inches apart.

Cover the "filled" strip with another strip of pasta the same size.

Carefully, with your fingers, press the two strips of pasta together in between each mound of filling.

Seal the outside edges, and cut or press the individual ravioli apart. If the pasta seems difficult to seal, moisten the edges slightly with a little water.

Bring a large kettle of salted water to a boil, and cook the ravioli until they rise to the top—about 15 minutes.

Drain, and serve the ravioli with grated Parmesan cheese or a marinara sauce. They can also be frozen and reheated in a 350-degree oven, with or without sauce.

Serves 4 to 6.

FETTUCINE ALFREDO

This delectable noodle dish from Italy is very rich and filling, and thus serves quite adequately as a main dish, accompanied by a crisp green salad and hot Italian bread. As an appetizer, try serving melon and prosciutto.

PASTA:

1 tablespoon salt
½ pound medium-width noodles (or use homemade pasta recipe on page 118)

SAUCE:

½ cup butter
⅔ cup heavy cream
1¼ cup freshly grated Parmesan cheese
  Salt and freshly ground pepper to taste
  Chopped parsley for garnish

In a large kettle, bring 4 quarters of water with 1 tablespoon of salt to a boil.

Add the noodles and cook, uncovered, until tender—about 7 to 10 minutes; drain the noodles, and keep them warm.

Meanwhile, make the Alfredo sauce: Heat the butter and cream in a medium saucepan over low heat until the butter is melted. Remove from the heat.

Add 1 cup of the Parmesan cheese and salt and pepper to taste, stirring until the sauce is blended and smooth.

Place the drained noodles in a serving bowl, and add the sauce; toss with two spoons until noodles are evenly coated with the sauce.

Sprinkle the remaining cheese and the chopped parsley over the noodles and serve at once.

Serves 4.

EGGPLANT MOZZARELLA

This recipe makes a nice meatless main dish; it's a cinch to prepare, too.

---

1 medium eggplant (about 2 pounds)
½ cup flour
½ cup olive oil (approx.)
1 can (16 ounces) tomato sauce
1 teaspoon garlic salt
1 teaspoon oregano
1 cup grated Parmesan cheese
1 pound mozzarella cheese, thinly sliced

Wash the eggplant, and cut it into ½-inch slices. (It is not necessary to peel the eggplant as the peel is quite tasty when well cooked.)

Dredge the eggplant slices lightly in the flour.

Heat the olive oil in a large skillet, and quickly sauté the eggplant slices until golden-brown on both sides; remove the slices as they brown, and drain them on paper towels. Add more oil to the skillet as needed.

Place half of the eggplant slices on the bottom of a 2-quart casserole.

Top with half of the tomato sauce, and season with half the garlic salt and oregano.

Sprinkle half the Parmesan cheese on top of the tomato sauce, and place half the mozzarella slices on top.

Make a second layer, using the remaining ingredients in the order given above.

Bake the casserole, covered, at 350 degrees for 30 minutes, or until the sauce is bubbly and the cheese is melted.

Serves 4.

HINT

To eliminate the bitter taste from eggplant, soak the slices in salt water for 15 minutes; drain well, and then use in any given recipe.

EASY SOUFFLÉ

Foolproof! Hardly anyone will be able to notice the difference between this and the real thing. It makes a nice dish for either a light supper or a Sunday brunch. For variety, add a little chopped ham.

---

6 slices white bread
1 cup grated cheddar cheese
3 eggs
2 cups milk
   Pinch of salt
   Freshly ground pepper to taste
1½ teaspoons dry mustard
4 drops of Tabasco sauce

The day before serving, cut the bread into 1-inch cubes, and place on the bottom of a buttered casserole.

Sprinkle the grated cheese over the bread.

In a medium bowl, beat together the eggs, milk, and seasonings.

Pour this mixture over the cheese.

Cover the casserole with foil, and refrigerate overnight.

One-half hour before baking, remove the casserole from the refrigerator, and let it warm up to room temperature.

Bake the casserole, uncovered, at 400 degrees for 55 minutes, or until the top is puffy and golden-brown.

Serves 4 to 6.

SPANAKOPITA

You should try fixing this Greek spinach-and-cheese pie for the first time on a lazy day when you feel like experimenting. Once you have mastered the recipe, you'll find it to be a perfect buffet dish.

---

2 pounds fresh spinach, or 2 packages (10 ounces each) frozen chopped spinach
¼ cup olive oil
½ cup finely chopped onion
2 tablespoons finely chopped shallots
¼ cup finely chopped scallions
¼ cup finely chopped parsley
2 tablespoons dried dill weed
¼ teaspoon salt
⅛ teaspoon freshly ground pepper
⅓ cup milk
¾ pound feta cheese, finely crumbled (available at Greek specialty stores)
4 eggs, lightly beaten
2 cups melted butter (approx.)
16 sheets (½ pound) filo pastry (available at Greek specialty stores)

If using fresh spinach, wash it thoroughly, discarding the stems. Chop the leaves and dry them well. If using frozen spinach, cook it according to package directions, and drain it thoroughly; set aside.

In a large skillet, heat the oil over medium heat.

Add the onion, shallots, and scallions; cook for 5 minutes, stirring frequently.

Stir in the chopped spinach; cover the skillet tightly, and cook for 5 minutes more.

Add the parsley, dill weed, salt, and pepper, stirring and shaking the pan constantly.

Cook, uncovered, for 10 minutes, or until the liquid evaporates and the spinach begins to stick to the skillet.

Transfer the mixture to a deep bowl, and add the milk; cool to room temperature. Add the cheese, and slowly beat in the eggs; set aside.

Preheat the oven to 300 degrees.

Clarify the melted butter by removing the milky residue on the top.

Use 2 tablespoons of the melted butter to coat the bottom and sides of a 9 × 13 × 2-inch baking pan.

Line the pan with a sheet of filo, being sure to press it into the corners and against the sides of the pan.

Brush the entire surface of the filo with 2 tablespoons of butter, and lay another sheet of filo on top.

Spread it with 2 more tablespoons of butter, and continue with filo and butter for 8 layers.

With a rubber scraper, spread the spinach mixture evenly over the eighth layer of filo, and smooth it into the corners.

Place another sheet of filo over the spinach, and brush it with melted butter; repeat as before with the remaining filo and melted butter.

Trim off the excess pastry from the sides. Brush the top piece of filo with the remaining butter. The dish may be frozen at this point if desired.

Bake, uncovered, for 1 hour. If baking directly from the freezer, increase the baking time to 1½ hours.

To serve, cut into squares; serve hot or lukewarm.

Serves 12.

MUSHROOM QUICHE

PASTRY:

1 cup sifted all-purpose flour (sift before measuring)
  Pinch of salt
⅓ cup vegetable shortening
3 to 4 tablespoons of ice water

FILLING:

4 tablespoons butter, softened
2 tablespoons finely chopped shallots
1 pound mushrooms, wiped clean and thinly sliced
1 teaspoon salt
1 teaspoon lemon juice
4 eggs
1 cup heavy cream
  Pinch of nutmeg
½ cup grated Swiss cheese

To prepare the pastry, sift the flour and salt together into a medium bowl.

Using a pastry blender or two knives, cut the shortening into the flour until the mixture resembles coarse cornmeal.

Slowly sprinkle the ice water over the top of the mixture while tossing it with a fork.

Gather the dough into a ball, and press it with the heel of your hand. Add only enough additional ice water to bind the dough together.

Remake the ball, wrap it in waxed paper, and flatten it with your hand. Refrigerate the dough for 25 to 30 minutes.

Preheat the oven to 400 degrees.

Place the chilled dough on a lightly floured surface. With a rolling pin, roll the dough out from the center in all directions into a circle 11 or 12 inches in diameter.

Fit the dough into a 10-inch quiche pan or a 9-inch glass pie pan, crimping or fluting the top edges.

Place a piece of waxed paper over the dough, and fill it with pie weights or beans. (This keeps the dough from puffing up during baking. You can later "recycle" the beans for the same purpose.)

Bake the pastry for 6 to 8 minutes. Remove it to a wire rack to cool. The pastry may be frozen at this point. (When using frozen pastry, do not defrost it; just fill with desired filling and bake.)

Lower the oven heat to 350 degrees.

In a large skillet, melt 2 tablespoons of the butter; add the shallots, and cook for 2 minutes.

Stir in the mushrooms, salt, and lemon juice.

Cover the skillet and simmer over low heat for 10 minutes.

Uncover the skillet, increase the heat, and boil for 5 minutes, stirring frequently, until all the liquid has evaporated.

Rub the bottom of the cooled pastry shell with 1 tablespoon of the butter.

In a large bowl, beat the eggs and cream together, and add the nutmeg.

Stir in the mushrooms, and pour the mixture into the prepared shell.

Sprinkle the cheese on the top, and dot with the remaining butter.

Bake the quiche for 35 minutes, or until it is puffy and brown and a knife inserted in the center comes out clean. Cut in wedges and serve immediately.

Serves 4 to 6.

HINTS

Ice water makes any pie or pastry crust flakier.

Pure vegetable shortening or lard is best to use with pie dough; butter imparts a better flavor, but it melts too easily when the dough is being handled.

When making any pie or pastry dough, try to handle it as little as possible. Overhandling activates the gluten in the flour, making the resulting dough elastic. This is fine for yeast breads, but it tends to make pastry crusts tough instead of flaky.

MUSHROOM SOUFFLÉ

---

1 cup milk
3 tablespoons cornstarch mixed with 3 tablespoons water
½ teaspoon salt
⅛ teaspoon nutmeg
2 tablespoons butter
1 small onion, finely chopped
½ pound mushrooms, finely chopped
6 eggs, separated
¾ cup grated Gruyère or Swiss cheese

Butter a 2-quart soufflé dish, and place a buttered waxed paper collar around the top edge.

Preheat the oven to 375 degrees.

In a small saucepan scald the milk.

Add the cornstarch mixture and cook over low heat, stirring constantly, until the mixture is thickened.

Add the salt and nutmeg; remove the pan from the heat, transfer the mixture to a large bowl; set aside.

In a medium skillet melt the butter, and sauté the onion and the mushrooms for 2 minutes over medium-high heat.

Remove from the heat and drain off any excess liquid.

Place the sautéed onions and mushroom in a blender container with the egg yolks and puree until smooth; add the puree to the cornstarch mixture.

Add the cheese to the mushroom-cornstarch mixture.

In a deep bowl, with an electric mixer at high speed, beat the egg whites until stiff and fold them into the mushroom mixture.

Place the mixture in the prepared soufflé dish and bake it for 35 minutes, or until puffed and golden-brown. Serve immediately.

Serves 6 to 8.

MANICOTTI

Real manicotti are made with delicate crêpes, instead of those starchy shells you buy at the supermarket; and it makes all the difference in the world. Even dyed-in-the-wool meat eaters will agree that this recipe makes a satisfying meatless main dish.

CRÊPES:

1¼ cups water
 5 eggs
1¼ cups flour
    Pinch of salt
 1 teaspoon melted butter
    Additional melted butter for making crêpes

SAUCE:

 ¼ cup olive oil
 1 cup finely chopped onion
 1 garlic clove, crushed
 1 can (35 ounces) Italian plum tomatoes, with the liquid
 1 can (6 ounces) tomato paste
 3 tablespoons chopped parsley
2¼ teaspoons sugar
1½ teaspoons oregano
 ½ teaspoon basil
 ½ teaspoon salt
    Freshly ground pepper to taste

FILLING:

 2 pounds ricotta cheese
 ½ pound diced mozzarella cheese
 ½ cup grated Parmesan cheese
 2 tablespoons chopped parsley
    Salt and freshly ground pepper to taste

To make the crêpes, place the water, eggs, flour, salt, and melted butter in a blender container, and blend until smooth.

Heat a 7- or 8-inch crêpe pan over medium heat for a few minutes.

Brush the pan with a little melted butter.

Pour in just enough batter to cover the bottom of the pan (about 3 tablespoons). Cook the crêpe until it is dry on top and barely light brown on the bottom. (Do not let them brown as you would dessert crêpes.)

Turn the crêpe, and cook it until it is dry—about 30 seconds.

Remove the crêpe onto a wire rack, and repeat the process. Makes about 30 crêpes.

To make the sauce, heat the olive oil in a large skillet, and sauté the onion and garlic.

Add all the remaining sauce ingredients, and bring to a boil.

Lower the heat and simmer, covered, for 1 hour. This sauce can be used in any recipe calling for a marinara sauce; it freezes nicely, too.

In a large bowl, combine the ricotta, diced mozzarella, and ⅓ cup of the Parmesan. (Reserve the rest of the Parmesan for garnish.)

Add the parsley, and salt and pepper to taste.

To assemble the manicotti, pour some of the sauce in the bottom of a large shallow baking dish.

Place approximately 1½ tablespoons of the cheese filling in the center of each crêpe; fold it in thirds, and place it, seam side down, in the baking dish.

Cover the crêpes with the remaining sauce, and sprinkle the remaining Parmesan cheese on top. The dish can be assembled in advance to this point and frozen or refrigerated until needed.

Bake the manicotti, uncovered, at 350 degrees for 30 minutes. Remove the pan to a wire rack to cool for 5 minutes before serving.

If baking the manicotti directly from the freezer, bake at 350 degrees for 1 hour, or until thoroughly heated.

Serve with tossed salad and Italian bread.

Serves 10 to 12.

BEST BLINTZES EVER

Take your choice of two flavorful fillings and serve these for a light dinner or as a side dish.

BLINTZES:

 4 eggs
⅔ cup milk
⅔ cup water
 2 tablespoons vegetable oil
½ teaspoon salt
1⅓ cups flour
¼ cup melted butter (for cooking blintzes)

CHEESE FILLING:

12 ounces creamed cottage cheese
 2 tablespoons sugar
 1 teaspoon cinnamon
 1 teaspoon grated lemon peel
   Pinch of salt
 1 cup raisins

POTATO FILLING:

 4 tablespoons butter or margarine
 2 or 3 large onions, finely chopped
 3 cups mashed potatoes
   Salt and freshly ground pepper to taste

 1 to 2 tablespoons butter for cooking filled blintzes

To prepare the blintzes, beat the eggs well in a medium bowl.
Add the milk, water, oil, salt, and flour, stirring well.
Let the mixture stand at room temperature for 1 to 2 hours.

Place a 7- or 8-inch crêpe pan over medium heat for about 3 minutes.

Brush the pan with a little melted butter.

Lift the pan from the heat and add enough batter to cover the bottom (about 3 tablespoons); tilt the pan to spread the batter evenly.

Cook the blintz over medium heat until it is slightly golden on the bottom.

Turn it over and cook the other side in the same way; do not let it brown.

Slide the blintz from the pan onto a dish; cover it with a towel to keep it warm.

Brush the pan with melted butter and repeat the process until all the batter is used.

To make the cheese filling, place the cottage cheese in a strainer or colander and shake out all the excess liquid.

Combine the cheese with the remaining filling ingredients in a small bowl.

To make the potato filling, melt the butter in a large skillet and sauté the onions until soft but not brown.

Combine the sautéed onions with the mashed potatoes and salt and pepper in a medium bowl.

To fill the blintzes, place about 2 tablespoons of the desired filling in the center of each blintz.

Fold the sides into the center and then fold the other two sides into the center to make a neat rectangular package.

Filled blintzes may be refrigerated or frozen at this point.

A few minutes before serving, heat the butter in a large skillet.

Add the filled blintzes and gently brown them on both sides.

Serve at once with sour cream, strawberries or applesauce.

Serves 6.

BLINTZ SOUFFLÉ

A fabulous main dish for a Sunday brunch, or serve this as a side dish at the buffet table.

---

   4 tablespoons butter or margarine
  12 frozen cheese blintzes defrosted (Use homemade blintzes
     from preceding recipe, or buy the pre-cooked variety.)
   4 eggs
1¾ cups sour cream
  ¼ cup sugar
  ½ teaspoon salt
   1 teaspoon vanilla
   1 tablespoon orange juice

Grease a 9 × 9 × 2-inch baking pan.

Place the butter in the prepared pan and place the pan in a 350-degree oven until the butter is melted.

Remove the pan from the oven and arrange the defrosted blintzes in the bottom.

In a medium bowl combine the eggs, sour cream, sugar, salt, vanilla, and the orange juice, beating well.

Pour the mixture over the blintzes and bake, uncovered, for 45 minutes.

To serve, cut into squares.

The soufflé can stand at room temperature a few minutes before serving, but it will deflate.

Serves 6.

Chapter 3
ACCOMPANIMENTS

Rice & Noodles

Vegetables & Fruit

Potatoes

Many a cook who will brazenly whip up a soufflé or Steak Diane will avoid making rice from scratch, fearing that it will not come out right and opting instead for the more costly, cottony instant rice.

Regardless of the recipe, it is not difficult to cook raw rice. When serving it plain, always cook for the exact amount of time specified on the package. If the rice is too moist or too dry after the prescribed cooking time has elapsed, adjust the heat accordingly the next time you fix it. Do not lift the pot lid or stir the rice while it is cooking; this interferes with the proper circulation of the steam.

Long-grain rice costs more than medium- or short-grain, but its flavor and texture are superior. Converted white rice keeps for long periods without danger of weevil infestation. When cooked, each grain remains separate and stays that way whether you keep it warm for serving or leave it in the refrigerator. Converted rice is also more nutritious than ordinary white race because the vitamin B content is retained.

Rice and Noodles

CHINESE OVEN RICE

This is an excellent accompaniment to any Chinese- or Polynesian-style main dish, but it goes equally well with veal, steak, and chicken. It is truly a foolproof recipe.

---

2 cups long-grain white rice
¼ cup salad oil
3 tablespoons soy sauce
1 package dry onion-soup mix
1 can (8 ounces) sliced mushrooms
3½ cups water (approx.)

In a 2-quart casserole, combine the rice, oil, soy sauce, and onion-soup mix.

Drain the liquid from mushrooms into a four-cup measure. Add the mushrooms to the rice mixture.

Add enough water to the mushroom liquid to measure four cups, and pour into the casserole, mixing well.

Cover and bake at 350 degrees for 1 hour.

If not serving right away, turn off the oven, and leave the rice standing in it, covered. It will stay hot for up to one hour without drying out.

Serves 8 to 10.

Note: *For a different flavor, substitute dry beef-mushroom soup mix for onion-soup mix; eliminate the canned mushrooms, and use 4 cups of water.*

RISOTTO À LA MILANESE I

A classic Italian dish that is rich, buttery, and absolutely irresistible. Serve with veal or chicken.

---

1 can (10½ ounces) condensed chicken broth, undiluted
6 tablespoons butter
1 medium onion, finely chopped
1 cup long-grain white rice
½ cup water
⅓ cup dry white wine or vermouth
½ cup freshly grated Parmesan cheese

In a small saucepan, heat the chicken broth just until hot; set aside.

Melt 4 tablespoons of the butter in a heavy skillet, and sauté the onion until tender, but not brown.

Add the rice, and cook, stirring occasionally, until rice is golden—about 5 minutes.

Add the chicken broth, water, and wine; bring to a boil.

Reduce heat and simmer, covered, for 30 minutes, or until all liquid is absorbed.

Rice may be made up to an hour in advance to this point and kept warm on the stove. Just before serving, stir in the remaining butter and cheese, blending well to melt the cheese.

Serves 4 to 6.

RISOTTO À LA MILANESE II

This version has a slightly more full-bodied taste, and as such, it goes very well with steak.

---

     2 cups long-grain white rice
 1½ teaspoons saffron
     2 cans (10½ ounces each) condensed beef bouillon, un-
         diluted
 1½ cups water (approx.)
     1 teaspoon bottled beef extract
     2 cups freshly grated Parmesan cheese
   ½ cup melted butter

Place the rice in 2-quart saucepan, and crumble in the saffron.

Pour both cans of beef bouillon into a four-cup measure; add enough water to measure four cups.

Add this mixture to rice, along with beef extract. Bring to a boil, stirring occasionally.

Reduce heat, cover, and simmer to 20 to 25 minutes, or until the liquid is absorbed.

This recipe may be made in advance up to this point and kept warm on the stove. Just before serving, stir in one cup of the cheese and the melted butter, mixing well to melt cheese. Pass remaining cheese separately.

Serves 6 to 8.

WILD RICE CASSEROLE

By law, wild rice is harvested exclusively by Indians in the northern Plains states. It is really a grain, not a rice, and is quite expensive, almost a delicacy. For special dinners it adds just the right touch.

---

    4 tablespoons butter
    3 tablespoons chopped onion
    3 tablespoons chopped celery (optional)
    ½ pound mushrooms, wiped clean and sliced
    1 cup wild rice
    1 cup long-grain white rice
    4 chicken bouillon cubes dissolved in 1 quart boiling water
    3 tablespoons soy sauce
    ½ teaspoon salt

In a skillet, melt the butter, and sauté the onion, celery, and mushrooms until tender but not brown—about 5 minutes.

Place vegetables in a 2-quart casserole, along with the remaining ingredients, mixing well.

Cover, and bake for 40 minutes at 350 degrees.

Uncover the casserole, and bake an additional 15 minutes.

If not serving right away, turn off the oven and cover the casserole. The rice can stand in the oven for up to 1 hour.

Serves 6 to 8.

Remember: *1 stick of butter or margarine = ¼ pound = ½ cup = 8 tablespoons.*

CREAMY NOODLE CASSEROLE

A perfect accompaniment to pot roast or, with a tossed salad, a light meal in itself.

½ pound medium-width egg noodles
 2 cups creamed cottage cheese
 2 cups sour cream
¼ cup melted butter or margarine
¼ cup finely chopped onion
 1 clove garlic, minced
 1 teaspoon Worcestershire sauce
    Dash of Tabasco sauce
    Salt and freshly ground pepper to taste
    Freshly grated Parmesan cheese (optional)

Cook the noodles in 4 quarts of boiling salted water for 10 minutes.

Drain, and rinse with cold water.

In a large bowl, combine the remaining ingredients except the Parmesan cheese, mixing well.

Stir in the noodles, mixing until thoroughly combined.

Transfer the mixture to a buttered 2-quart casserole.

The recipe may be made in advance to this point and refrigerated until needed.

Bake the noodles, uncovered, at 350 degrees for 45 minutes, or until the sauce is bubbly. Serve hot, accompanied by grated Parmesan cheese, if desired.

Serves 8.

Vegetables and Fruit

RATATOUILLE

Pronounced "rah-tah-too-wee," this vegetable mixture is a specialty of the Provence region of France, an area noted for its robust, flavorful cuisine. It can be served hot, at room temperature, or cold.

---

3 green peppers
1 eggplant (about 1½ pounds)
1 small zucchini
3 tablespoons olive oil
4 cloves garlic, crushed
1 tablespoon finely chopped shallots
1 large Spanish onion, sliced
6 tomatoes, peeled and coarsely chopped
1 can (6 ounces) tomato paste
   Salt and freshly ground pepper to taste
   Pinch of cayenne pepper
2 teaspoons finely chopped parsley

Wash and seed the green peppers, and slice them into 1-inch strips.

Cut the eggplant and zucchini into 1-inch cubes. (It is not necessary to peel them.) Set aside.

Heat the olive oil in a large skillet, and add the green pepper, garlic, and shallots. Cook over medium-low heat for 5 minutes.

Add the sliced onion, and cook about 3 more minutes, stirring.

Add the remaining ingredients, mixing well.

Cover, and cook over low heat for 1 hour, or until the eggplant and zucchini are tender and mixture is thick. Stir occasionally during cooking time, and correct the seasonings to taste.

If not serving right away, refrigerate the mixture in covered dish. It will keep for several days in the refrigerator and can be reheated if desired.

Serves 4 to 6.

ZUCCHINI ITALIAN STYLE

A distant cousin of ratatouille, but with fewer ingredients. It is best to fix this dish early in the day and leave it standing, covered, for several hours. Quickly reheat just before serving.

¼ cup olive oil
1 medium onion, chopped
1 can (16 ounces) whole tomatoes, undrained, *or* 4 fresh
   tomatoes, peeled and halved
½ teaspoon dried basil
   Salt and freshly ground pepper to taste
4 medium zucchini
2 eggs
½ cup grated Parmesan cheese

In a 3-quart saucepan, heat the oil over medium heat, and sauté the onion until golden.

Add the tomatoes, basil, and salt and pepper to taste; simmer, covered, for 30 minutes.

Meanwhile, cut the zucchini into ½-inch slices; then cut the slices into quarters. Add to the tomato mixture.

Beat the eggs, and swirl into the pot. Cook, covered, for 15 minutes.

Add the cheese, mixing well, and cook another 5 minutes.

Let the mixture stand at room temperature for several hours. Reheat just before serving.

Serves 4 to 6.

HINT

Dried herbs are more concentrated than fresh ones. If a given recipe calls for dried herbs, you may substitute the fresh variety by doubling the amount indicated. Conversely, if a recipe calls for fresh herbs, use half the amount of dried herbs.

OLD-FASHIONED CORN PUDDING

In the summer, if you have leftover cooked corn-on-the-cob, remove the kernels and use them in this tasty recipe. Other times of the year, canned corn can be used.

---

  3 eggs
½ cup milk or light cream
     Salt and freshly ground pepper to taste
     Pinch of nutmeg
  2 cups fresh cooked corn (you will need 3 to 4 ears of corn), *or* 1 can (12 ounces) niblet corn, drained
½ cup grated Swiss cheese (optional)

In a medium bowl, beat the eggs until frothy.

Add the milk or cream and seasonings.

Stir in the corn and optional cheese.

Turn the mixture into a buttered 1-quart casserole, and bake at 325 degrees for 30 to 35 minutes, or until a knife inserted in the center comes out clean.

Serves 4.

Note: For an interesting flavour variation, add ¼ cup sautéed chopped onions or mushrooms, or a peeled and chopped tomato.

MUSHROOMS FLORENTINE

Whenever you see the word "Florentine" in a recipe or on a menu, it means that chopped spinach is one of the primary ingredients. The following recipe is simple to prepare and is ideally suited for buffet serving.

½ cup butter or margarine
1 pound mushrooms, wiped clean and sliced
2 packages (10 ounces each) frozen chopped spinach, thawed
    and well drained
  Salt and freshly ground pepper to taste
  Pinch of garlic salt
1 cup grated cheddar cheese

Melt 4 tablespoons of the butter in a large skillet, and sauté the mushrooms over medium heat until tender—about 10 minutes—stirring occasionally.

Line a large shallow ovenproof dish with the thawed and drained spinach. Sprinkle with the salt, pepper, and garlic salt.

Melt the remaining butter, and drizzle over the spinach.

Sprinkle ½ cup of cheese over this, and top with the sautéed mushrooms.

Cover with the remaining cheese.

This recipe may be made in advance up to this point and refrigerated until needed.

Bake, uncovered, at 350 degrees for 20 minutes, or until the cheese is melted and bubbly.

Serves 8.

Remember: *¼ pound of hard cheese (cheddar, Swiss, Parmesan) will yield 1 cup of grated cheese.*

ARTICHOKE-SPINACH CASSEROLE

---

4 jars (6 ounces each) marinated artichoke hearts, drained
3 packages (10 ounces each) frozen chopped spinach, par-
    tially defrosted
2 packages (8 ounces each) cream cheese, softened
5 tablespoons butter or margarine, softened
¾ cup milk
⅔ cup grated Parmesan cheese

The day before serving grease a 9 × 13 × 2-inch baking pan.

Slice or coarsely chop the artichoke hearts and place them in the prepared pan.

Squeeze the spinach to remove all excess liquid and place the spinach over the artichokes.

In a medium bowl, with an electric mixer at medium speed, blend the cream cheese and butter until smooth and fluffy.

Gradually add the milk, blending until smooth.

Pour this mixture over the spinach and sprinkle the Parmesan cheese on top.

Cover, and refrigerate for 24 hours.

Bake the casserole, uncovered, at 350 degrees for 40 to 45 minutes, or until top is bubbly.

To serve, cut into squares.

Serves 12.

SWEET AND SOUR ASPARAGUS

1 can (14½ ounces) asparagus spears, drained
¼ cup wine vinegar
½ cup sugar
¼ cup water
½ teaspoon celery seed
1 cinnamon stick
3 whole cloves
½ teaspoon salt

One day or more before serving, place the drained asparagus spears in a shallow refrigerator dish.

Combine the remaining ingredients in a small saucepan, and cook over medium heat for 5 minutes.

Pour the hot liquid over the asparagus, cover, and refrigerate overnight or longer.

Before serving, discard the cinnamon stick and cloves.

Serves 4.

HINT

When cooking with vinegar, always use a glass, enamel, or stainless-steel saucepan. Aluminum pans react with the vinegar, causing an unpleasant metallic taste.

OYSTER GREEN BEANS

A novel recipe that will perk up vegetable-weary appetites.

½ teaspoon seasoned salt
2 tablespoons wine vinegar
½ teaspoon garlic powder
1 can (3½ ounces) smoked oysters, packed in oil
  Salt and freshly ground pepper to taste
3 cans (16 ounces each) whole green beans, well drained
1 medium red onion, thinly sliced
2 tablespoons peanut oil

The day before serving, stir together the seasoned salt, vinegar, and garlic powder in a large bowl.

Add the oysters along with their oil, and blend well.

Season with the salt and pepper to taste.

Add the green beans, onion, and peanut oil. Toss well to coat the beans with oil and seasonings.

Cover, and refrigerate overnight. Serve chilled.

Serves 8 to 10.

CARROT CAKE RING

This "cake" is a delightful side dish, especially at a buffet dinner. After unmolding the ring, you can fill the middle with cooked and drained peas mixed with sliced fresh mushrooms.

¾ cup shortening
2 eggs, separated
½ cup packed brown sugar

1 teaspoon lemon juice
1 tablespoon cold water
1½ cups grated carrots
1 cup flour
½ teaspoon baking soda
1 teaspoon baking powder
½ teaspoon salt
½ cup unseasoned bread crumbs (approx.)

In a large bowl, with an electric mixer at medium speed, cream together the shortening, egg yolks, and brown sugar, beating until smooth and fluffy.

Add the lemon juice, water, and carrots, blending well.

Sift together the flour, baking soda, baking powder, and salt, and add to the carrot mixture; mix well.

Preheat the oven to 375 degrees.

Wash and dry the beaters thoroughly, and in a small deep bowl, beat the egg whites until stiff.

Fold into the batter until thoroughly incorporated.

Butter a 9-inch ring pan, and sprinkle with the bread crumbs to obtain a thin coating all around the pan; shake off any excess.

Pour in the batter, and bake 40 to 45 minutes, or until nicely browned on top.

Cool the cake on a wire rack 15 minutes before turning it out of the pan.

This recipe may be frozen and reheated, wrapped in foil.

Serves 8 to 10.

HINT

When a recipe calls for shortening, use pure white vegetable shortening. In a pinch margarine can be substituted, but unless it's unsalted, it will make the recipe taste saltier. Never use liquid shortening or oil in place of vegetable shortening.

TOMATO-CHEESE MELANGE

A very easy and flavorful dish.

---

2 cans (28 ounces each) whole tomatoes, drained and coarsely chopped
2 cups grated cheddar cheese
3 cups unseasoned croutons
3 medium onions, thinly sliced
1½ teaspoons garlic salt
½ teaspoon dried oregano
2½ teaspoons sugar
2 tablespoons butter or margarine

Place one-third of the tomatoes in the bottom of a 2-quart casserole.

Top the tomatoes with one-fourth of the cheese.

Place one-third of the croutons over cheese.

Layer one-third of the onion slices on top of the croutons.

Combine the seasonings and sugar, and sprinkle one-third of this mixture over croutons.

Repeat, making three layers, and ending with the remaining one-fourth of cheese.

Dot with butter.

This recipe may be made ahead and refrigerated at this point.

Bake, uncovered, at 350 degrees for 30 minutes, or until the cheese is bubbly.

Serves 6 to 8.

HINT

Tomatoes cut vertically "bleed" less.

CHEESE SOUFFLÉ BAKED IN TOMATOES

Since these must be baked immediately before serving, you should have your main dish already prepared. If you serve a roast, you can remove it from the oven just before baking the tomatoes; cover the meat with foil and it will keep warm until serving time. These miniature soufflés can also be served for a light lunch or brunch.

---

     6 firm medium-sized tomatoes
       Salt and freshly ground pepper to taste
1½ tablespoons butter or margarine
     1 tablespoon flour
     ¼ cup light cream
     ¼ tablespoon salt
       Dash of cayenne pepper
     ¼ teaspoon dried tarragon
     1 cup grated Gruyère or Swiss cheese
     3 eggs, separated

Slice off the tomato tops and scoop out the pulp, being careful not to break the shells. (Pulp may be used to make tomato sauce, if desired.)

Sprinkle the insides of the tomatoes with salt and pepper to taste.

Preheat the oven to 350 degrees.

Melt the butter in a small saucepan and stir in the flour.

Over low heat gradually add the cream, salt, cayenne, and tarragon.

Cook, stirring constantly, until the sauce is thick and smooth; remove from the heat and stir in the cheese.

Let the sauce cool a few minutes; then beat in the egg yolks.

In a deep bowl, with an electric mixer at high speed, beat the egg whites until stiff and fold them into the cheese mixture.

Spoon the mixture into the tomato shells, filling each about two-thirds full.

Place the tomatoes in a greased shallow baking pan and bake them for 15 to 20 minutes, or until the soufflé is puffed and golden-brown.

Serve immediately.

Serves 6.

CURRIED FRUIT COMPOTE

Fruit can often be served instead of (or in addition to) vegetables as a main-dish accompaniment. This dish goes especially well with baked ham or poultry and boiled white rice. It can also be served as a dessert.

---

1 can (16 ounces) pears, drained
1 can (20 ounces) sliced pineapple, drained
1 can (16 ounces) peach halves, drained
1 can (8¾ ounces) apricots, drained, *or* 1 cup dried apricots
1 jar (4 ounces) maraschino cherries, drained
⅓ cup butter or margarine
⅔ cup packed dark brown sugar
2 teaspoons curry powder

Place the drained fruits in a 2-quart casserole.

Melt the butter in a small saucepan, and add the sugar and curry powder, stirring until well blended.

Pour the butter mixture over the fruits.

This recipe may be made in advance to this point and refrigerated until needed.

Bake, uncovered, at 325 degrees for 1 hour. Any leftovers can be gently reheated on top of the stove.

Serves 8 to 10.

Potatoes

HAWAIIAN SWEET POTATOES

Sweet and delicious. Try them with roast turkey or baked ham.

---

   6 sweet potatoes, washed and cut in half lengthwise (do *not* peel)
 ⅓ cup sugar
 ½ cup butter or margarine, softened
   1 teaspoon cinnamon
   1 can (8 ounces) crushed pineapple
 ½ cup chopped pecans
 ⅓ cup packed brown sugar
   2 tablespoons additional butter or margarine

Boil the halved potatoes in water to cover until tender— about 30 minutes. Drain well.

Scoop out the pulp, and place it in a large bowl; keep the shells intact.

Mash the pulp, and add the sugar, butter, and cinnamon.

Drain the pineapple, reserving the liquid.

Add the pineapple to the potatoes, along with the pecans, mixing well.

Dip the empty potato shells in the reserved pineapple juice, and spoon the potato mixture into the shells.

Sprinkle the brown sugar over the potatoes, and dot with butter.

Place the filled shells in a large greased baking dish.

This recipe may be made in advance to this point.

Bake at 350 degrees 15 to 20 minutes, or until potatoes are thoroughly heated.

Serves 8 to 12.

POTATOES TARRAGON

3 large baking potatoes
6 tablespoons unsalted butter
1 tablespoon dried tarragon

Peel the potatoes, and scoop them with a melon baller into small balls.

Place the potatoes in a saucepan with salted water to cover; bring to a boil.

Boil 10 to 15 minutes, or until the potato balls are tender but not mushy. (Cooking time depends on the size of the balls.)

Drain the potatoes. If not serving right away, the potato balls may be refrigerated at this point.

About 5 minutes before serving, melt the butter in a large skillet, and sauté the potatoes over medium heat for about 3 minutes.

Sprinkle with the tarragon, toss well, and serve immediately.

Serves 4.

RULE OF THUMB

Any vegetable that grows underground (potatoes, beets, carrots, etc.) should start cooking in cold water. Vegetables that grow aboveground (peas, beans, corn, etc.) should start cooking in boiling water.

SINFUL POTATOES

Not only is this dish quick and easy to prepare, but it can also be made in advance and frozen until needed. What's more, it will feed an army! Because it is so rich, small portions will suffice. Halve the recipe if you like, or double it for those extra-large gatherings.

½ pound bacon
1 package (2 pounds) frozen hash-brown potatoes
1 pound Velveeta cheese
2 cups mayonnaise

Cook the bacon in a large skillet until crisp and brown. Drain it well on paper towels and crumble it into small pieces.

Slightly defrost the potatoes—about 15 minutes.

In a heavy saucepan, over low heat, melt the Velveeta, stirring constantly.

Combine the melted cheese, mayonnaise, and potatoes in a large bowl, mixing well.

Transfer mixture to a large shallow baking dish, and top with the crumbled bacon.

This recipe may be made in advance to this point and refrigerated or frozen until needed.

Bake, uncovered, at 350 degrees for 35 to 40 minutes, or until bubbly and golden-brown. If baking directly from freezer, increase baking time to 1 hour.

Serves 24.

ENERGY-SAVING TIP

You do not have to preheat the oven unless the recipe contains leavening ingredients (e.g., cakes, breads, rolls, biscuits), or unless you are using the broiler.

Chapter 4
·
SALADS

Vegetable Salads
Salad Dressings
Gelatin Salads

Vegetable Salads

CAESAR SALAD

The king of salads. Although it must be tossed at the last minute, all the ingredients can be readied in advance.

---

1 large head (about 2 pounds) romaine lettuce (no other kind)
1 egg
½ cup olive oil (no other kind)
2 garlic cloves, crushed
Salt and freshly ground pepper to taste
1 teaspoon dry mustard
¼ cup lemon juice
Dash of Worcestershire sauce
1 garlic clove (for seasoning bowl)
½ cup croutons
½ cup freshly grated Parmesan cheese
½ cup bleu cheese, crumbled
¼ cup chopped anchovies (optional)

Several hours before serving, wash and thoroughly dry the lettuce, and tear it into bite-sized pieces. Wrap it in a tea towel, and refrigerate until needed.

Coddle the egg by placing it in boiling water for 1 minute.

Crack the egg into a bowl, and add the olive oil, crushed garlic, salt and pepper to taste, mustard, lemon juice, and Worcestershire sauce; mix well with a wire whisk.

Place the dressing in a jar with a tight-fitting lid, and refrigerate.

Just before serving, split the remaining garlic clove and use it to rub the inside of a wooden salad bowl; discard the garlic.

Place the lettuce in the bowl, and add the croutons, Parmesan, and bleu cheese.

Shake the dressing in the jar to combine the ingredients, and add it to the salad, tossing thoroughly.

Garnish the salad with anchovies, if desired.

Serve immediately.

Serves 4 to 6.

_____ **HINT** _____

Salad greens should always be torn, never cut with a knife.

•

REFRIGERATOR SLAW

If you're tired of cole slaw made with mayonnaise, try this recipe for a different taste sensation. It also has the virtue of keeping much longer than cole slaw made with mayonnaise.

---

1 large head cabbage (about 3 pounds), shredded
1 large onion, thinly sliced
1 cup + 2 teaspoons sugar
¾ cup vegetable oil
1 scant tablespoon salt
1 teaspoon celery seed
1 teaspoon dry mustard
1 cup white vinegar

Two or more days before serving, layer the shredded cabbage and the sliced onion alternately in a large bowl.

Spread 1 cup of the sugar over the cabbage-onion mixture; do not mix.

Combine the remaining ingredients, including the 2 teaspoons of sugar, in a medium saucepan, and bring to a boil over high heat; let the mixture boil for 3 minutes.

Pour the hot dressing over the cabbage.

Cover the bowl, and let it stand at room temperature for 4 to 6 hours; press the mixture down with a wooden spoon several times.

Refrigerate the slaw, covered, for at least two days before serving. The slaw will keep for several weeks in the refrigerator.

Serves 8 to 10.

VEGETABLE BOUQUET

In the winter, when fresh vegetables are usually scarce and of poor quality, bring out this recipe. It is guaranteed to win high marks.

VEGETABLES:

    1 can (16 ounces) cut green beans, well drained
    1 can (16 ounces) red kidney beans, well drained
    1 can (7 ounces) pitted black olives, well drained
    1 can (8 ounces) button mushrooms, well drained
    1 can (15 ounces) artichoke hearts, well drained
    1 tablespoon diced pimiento (optional)
 1½ cups diagonally sliced celery
    1 medium onion, thinly sliced

DRESSING:

    ½ cup red wine vinegar
 1½ teaspoons MSG (optional)
 1¼ teaspoons salt
    1 teaspoon sugar

1 tablespoon dried *fines herbes*
¼ teaspoon Tabasco sauce
½ cup vegetable oil

GARNISH:

¼ cup chopped parsley
1 tablespoon capers (optional)

Several hours or the day before serving, combine the beans, olives, mushrooms, and artichoke hearts with the optional pimiento, celery, and onion in a large bowl.

To make the dressing, pour the vinegar into a bowl or a container.

Add the optional MSG, salt, and sugar, stirring to dissolve.

Add the *fines herbes*, Tabasco sauce, and oil; stir or shake until well blended.

Pour the dressing over the vegetables, and refrigerate, covered, several hours or overnight.

To serve, spoon the mixture into a large glass bowl (it looks more attractive that way), and garnish with parsley and the optional capers.

Serves 10 to 12.

HINT

It is not worth worrying whether an onion is medium- or large-sized in most recipes. The size is just given as a guideline, but you should always use your own good judgment.

TABOULEH

A unique salad from the Middle East.

---

1 cup cracked wheat (bulgur wheat)
2 large tomatoes, diced
¾ cup chopped scallions
¼ cup olive oil
⅓ to ½ cup fresh lemon juice
¾ cup chopped parsley
1 teaspoon salt
  Freshly ground pepper to taste
2 tablespoons dried mint leaves, *or* ¼ cup chopped fresh
  mint leaves

A few hours before serving, place the wheat in a large bowl, and cover it with boiling water; let it stand for 15 minutes. (The wheat should feel tender but slightly crunchy.)

Drain off the water, and wash the wheat under the faucet 2 or 3 more times; drain thoroughly.

In a salad bowl, combine the wheat with the tomatoes and scallions.

Add the oil, lemon juice, parsley, salt, and pepper to taste; stir to blend well.

Garnish with the mint leaves.

Cover the bowl, and refrigerate it for at least 2 hours before serving.

Serves 8.

24-HOUR SALAD

This delightful salad is made a day in advance and refrigerated until serving time—a boon to the busy host or hostess.

- 1 medium head iceberg lettuce
- 1 medium head cauliflower
- 1 pound bacon, fried until crisp, well drained
- 1½ cups mayonnaise
- 1 package mild Italian salad dressing mix
- 2 packages (10 ounces each) frozen peas
- ½ cup freshly grated Parmesan cheese

The day before serving, shred the lettuce and place it in a large bowl.

Remove the flowerettes from the cauliflower, and break them into very small pieces. Place them on top of the lettuce.

Crumble the bacon finely, and place it on top of the cauliflower.

Spread the mayonnaise evenly over these ingredients, and sprinkle the dressing mix over the mayonnaise.

Add the frozen peas, and sprinkle the grated Parmesan on top.

Cover the bowl tightly, and refrigerate overnight.

Just before serving, toss all the ingredients together.

Serves 12.

TOSSED ITALIAN SALAD

5 cups iceberg or romaine lettuce, torn into bite-sized pieces
1 package (10 ounces) frozen mixed vegetables, cooked, drained, and chilled
6 ounces mozzarella cheese, diced
1 cup garbanzo beans, drained
½ cup thinly sliced pepperoni
½ cup Italian salad dressing (homemade or bottled)
  Wine vinegar to taste

Place the lettuce in a plastic bag with about 12 ice cubes. Close the bag tightly, and refrigerate until needed.

Place the chilled mixed vegetables, cheese, beans, and pepperoni in another plastic bag; close it tightly, and refrigerate until needed.

Combine the Italian salad dressing with wine vinegar to taste in a jar with a tight-fitting lid. Shake well, and refrigerate until needed.

Just before serving, pour off the water from the lettuce, and place the lettuce in a large salad bowl.

Add the vegetable mixture to the lettuce, and combine well.

Add the dressing, and toss until thoroughly combined.

Serves 6 to 8.

CHUTNEY CHICKEN SALAD

Whether your party is indoors or outdoors, this recipe can't be beat. It's a delicious way to use up leftover chicken.

---

  1 cup mayonnaise
 ¼ cup chopped chutney
  1 teaspoon curry powder
  2 teaspoons grated lime peel
 ¼ cup fresh lime juice
 ¼ teaspoon salt
  4 cups diced cooked white chicken meat
  2 cans (13¼ ounces each) pineapple chunks, well drained
  2 cups diagonally sliced celery
 ½ cup finely chopped chives, *or* ¼ cup freeze-dried chives
 ½ cup slivered almonds, blanched and toasted

In a large bowl, combine the mayonnaise, chutney, curry powder, lime peel, lime juice, and salt, mixing well.

Add the remaining ingredients, mixing until they are thoroughly combined with the mayonnaise mixture.

Refrigerate the salad, covered, until serving. (It may be made up to one day in advance.)

To serve, mound the salad onto a serving platter lined with lettuce leaves.

Serves 4.

HINT

Don't discard the peels of citrus fruits; instead, grate them, place them in a tightly covered container, and store in the freezer to use as needed. When grating the peel of any citrus fruit, try not to use the inner white rind because it has a bitter taste. The peel of these fruits is sometimes called the "zest," and this is what imparts the citrus flavor to recipes.

SALAD NIÇOISE

A French-style chef's salad that's ideal for warm-weather enter-
taining.

DRESSING:

1 tablespoon dry mustard
1 teaspoon sugar
1 tablespoon salt
  Freshly ground black pepper to taste
2 garlic cloves, crushed
½ cup tarragon vinegar
¼ cup fresh lemon juice
2 cups olive oil

SALAD:

2 pounds new potatoes, peeled, boiled, and sliced
2 cups cooked cut green beans, canned, frozen, or fresh
1 cup canned or frozen artichoke hearts
1 large Spanish or Bermuda onion, very thinly sliced
1 head leafy lettuce (romaine, Boston, or chicory)
3 cans (6½ ounces each) white tuna, drained and flaked
1 pint cherry tomatoes
1 cup pitted black olives
6 hard-boiled eggs, quartered
½ cup pimiento, cut into strips
1 large green pepper, seeded and very thinly sliced
2 cans (2 ounces) rolled anchovies with capers, well drained
½ cup chopped parsley

Several hours before serving, make the dressing: In a large
jar or container with a tight-fitting lid, combine the mustard,
sugar, salt, and pepper to taste.

Mix in the garlic, vinegar, and lemon juice; shake well.

Add the oil, and shake well again. (This dressing can be

used for any tossed salad. Store it, tightly covered, in the refrigerator, and use as needed.)

In a large bowl, combine the potatoes, beans, artichoke hearts, and onion.

Add the dressing, and marinate the vegetables in the refrigerator for a few hours, stirring gently from time to time.

A few minutes before serving, line a large salad bowl with the lettuce.

Drain the marinated vegetables, reserving the dressing. Spoon the vegetables over the lettuce.

Place the tuna in the middle of the vegetables, and arrange the tomatoes, olives, eggs, pimiento, green pepper, and anchovies around the tuna.

Sprinkle the top lightly with the parsley.

Pass the reserved dressing separately, or mix it into the salad just before serving.

Serves 6 as a main dish, 12 as a side dish.

POTATO SALAD DELUXE

Although Idaho potatoes are not necessary to insure the success of this recipe, they are recommended because they have a firmer texture.

---

4 pounds Idaho potatoes

DRESSING:

1 small cucumber
1½ cups mayonnaise
1 large onion, finely chopped
1 stalk celery, finely chopped
1 hard-boiled egg, finely chopped
½ cup chopped sweet pickles
¼ cup sweet pickle juice
2 tablespoons cider or white vinegar
1½ teaspoons salt

The day before serving, place the unpeeled potatoes in a large kettle with salted water to cover. Bring to a boil, and cook exactly 30 minutes after the water reaches the boiling point.

Drain the potatoes, and place them in the refrigerator to cool.

Meanwhile, make the dressing: Peel the cucumber, and cut it in half lengthwise. Scoop out the seeds and discard. Chop the cucumber very finely.

In a small bowl, combine the chopped cucumber with the remaining ingredients; refrigerate, covered, for 1 hour.

When the potatoes are cool enough to handle, peel and dice them.

Mix the potatoes with the dressing, and refrigerate, covered, overnight.

Serves 8 to 10.

Salad Dressings

CHRISTMAS SALAD DRESSING

You don't have to wait until Christmas to try this delicious salad dressing. It will enhance even the most ordinary of salads.

---

  1 can (10¾ ounces) condensed tomato soup, undiluted
⅓ cup honey
    Pinch of salt
  1 tablespoon paprika
  2 teaspoons prepared mustard
  2 tablespoons chopped onion
¼ cup lemon juice
  2 tablespoons white vinegar
  1 tablespoon Worcestershire sauce
¾ cup vegetable oil
  1 garlic clove, cut in half

Place all of the ingredients, except for the oil and garlic, in a blender container, and blend at high speed.

With the blender motor still running, gradually add the oil; continue blending until it is well combined.

Pour the dressing into a jar or container with a tight-fitting lid.

Add the garlic.

Cover, and refrigerate; use as needed.

Makes about 3 cups.

POPPY-SEED DRESSING

This goes nicely with both vegetable and fruit salads.

---

1 cup sugar
½ cup cider vinegar
1 teaspoon salt
2 teaspoons dry mustard
¾ cup vegetable oil
1 tablespoon grated onion
1 tablespoon poppy seeds

In a small bowl, with a wire whisk, combine the sugar, vinegar, salt, and mustard, beating well until the sugar is dissolved. (The sugar must be thoroughly dissolved.)

Add the oil slowly, ¼ cup at a time, beating until the mixture is thick.

Add the onion and poppy seeds, blending well.

Cover, and refrigerate; use as needed.

Makes about 1½ cups.

BLEU CHEESE DRESSING

You will find this dressing superior to almost anything you can buy in a bottle. It keeps for up to 2 weeks in the refrigerator, and it tastes just as good with baked potatoes as it does with salads.

---

3 packages (4 ounces each) bleu cheese, crumbled
½ teaspoon Worcestershire sauce
1 tablespoon freshly ground pepper
2 cups mayonnaise
1 teaspoon garlic powder
1 tablespoon chopped chives
½ cup buttermilk (approx.)
1 cup sour cream

In a small bowl, with a wire whisk, combine all the ingredients except the buttermilk and sour cream.

Slowly add the buttermilk and sour cream, mixing well. If the dressing is too thick, add more buttermilk, a tablespoon at a time, to reach the desired consistency.

Cover, refrigerate; use as needed.

Makes about 3½ cups.

Note: Use less buttermilk, and you will have a wonderful dip for raw vegetables.

Gelatin Salads

CHEESE SOUFFLÉ SALAD

*This is an excellent recipe for people who don't care for sweet
molded salads.*

---

1 package (3 ounces) lemon gelatin
1 tablespoon unflavored gelatin
1 cup hot water
½ cup cold water
½ cup mayonnaise
1 tablespoon lemon juice
¾ teaspoon salt
3 to 4 drops Tabasco sauce
¾ cup grated cheddar cheese
3 to 4 hard-boiled eggs, finely chopped
½ cup diced celery
¼ cup diced green pepper
2 tablespoons diced pimiento
1 teaspoon grated onion

In a medium bowl, dissolve the lemon juice and the unflavored gelatin in the hot water, mixing well.

Add the cold water, mayonnaise, lemon juice, salt, and
Tabasco sauce, and blend well with an electric mixer at medium
speed.

Place the mixture in the freezer for 15 minutes, or until it is
firm one inch around the edges but soft in the middle.

Remove the mixture from the freezer, and with an electric
mixer at medium speed, beat it until it is fluffy.

Fold in the remaining ingredients, and transfer the mixture

to a 4-cup mold that has been rinsed in cold water. Chill until firm.

To serve, unmold onto a large platter lined with lettuce leaves. If desired, serve with a dressing made of equal parts of mayonnaise and sour cream.

Serves 8.

AVOCADO RING

Words fail to describe this heavenly molded salad. Even people who think they dislike avocado will find it divine!

---

2 envelopes unflavored gelatin
¼ cup cold water
1 cup unsweetened grapefruit juice
⅔ cup unsweetened orange juice
⅓ cup lemon juice
⅔ cup sugar
¾ teaspoon salt
1 cup finely chopped celery
¼ cup finely chopped onion
½ cup chopped walnuts (optional)
3 ripe avocados, well mashed

Soak the gelatin in the water for 5 minutes to soften it.

Meanwhile, place the grapefruit, orange, and lemon juices in a medium saucepan, and add the sugar and salt.

Bring the mixture to a boil, stirring constantly.

Remove from the heat, and add the gelatin; let it cool.

Add the celery, onion, and optional walnuts, stirring to blend well.

Stir in the mashed avocados, mix well, and pour into a 4-cup ring mold that has been rinsed in cold water.

Cover, and refrigerate several hours or overnight.

Just before serving, unmold the salad onto a serving platter lined with lettuce leaves. If desired, place cooked chicken, shrimp, or lobster inside the ring. Or, garnish it with tomatoes, cucumbers, and orange or grapefruit sections.

Serves 10 to 12.

JELLIED GAZPACHO SALAD

---

1 package (6 ounces) lemon gelatin
1½ cups boiling water
1¾ cups tomato juice cocktail (such as "V-8")
7 stalks of celery, finely chopped
4 medium tomatoes, peeled and chopped
6 scallions, finely chopped
1 cup stuffed olives, finely chopped
½ green pepper, finely chopped
¼ cup Italian-style salad dressing
1 package (8 ounces) cream cheese

The day before serving dissolve the lemon gelatin in the boiling water in a large bowl; let cool 15 minutes.

Add the tomato juice, stirring well, and chill the mixture until it is thickened—about 1 hour.

Add all of the chopped vegetables and the salad dressing to the gelatin mixture, blending well.

With a melon baller or a small scoop form the cream cheese into walnut-sized balls.

Place the cream cheese balls in a decorative manner in the

bottom of a 6-cup mold (so that they will be on top when the salad is unmolded).

Carefully pour the gelatin mixture over the cream cheese balls; cover, and refrigerate overnight.

To serve, unmold the salad onto a serving platter. If desired, garnish with lettuce leaves, tomato wedges, and cucumber slices.

Serves 10.

WINE MOLD

This can be made in an attractive bowl instead of a mold. It is a perfect buffet salad, and it tastes especially good with turkey, chicken, or ham. A guaranteed success.

---

1 package (6 ounces) cherry gelatin
2 cups boiling water
1 can (16 ounces) pitted dark cherries
½ cup dark cherry, black cherry, or other dark sweet wine (approx.)
1 cup wine (additional)
1 cup chopped walnuts (optional)

Dissolve the gelatin in the boiling water, stirring well.

Drain the cherries, pouring the liquid into a measuring cup. If the liquid does not measure 8 ounces, add enough wine to make 1 cup of liquid.

Add this juice to the gelatin, stirring well.

Add the cup of wine.

Stir in the cherries and walnuts, if desired.

Place the mixture in a 6-cup mold or an attractive serving

bowl, and refrigerate until set. The salad may be made one or two days ahead of time and kept in the refrigerator, tightly covered with foil.

If using a mold, just before serving, unmold the salad onto a serving platter lined with lettuce leaves.

Serves 8 to 10.

FROSTED SALAD

The kind of recipe you'll want to keep to yourself!

SALAD:

- 1 package (6 ounces) lemon gelatin
- 2 cups boiling water
- 2 cups lemon-lime soda
- 1 cup miniature marshmallows
- 1 can (20 ounces) crushed pineapple (reserve liquid for topping)
- 3 large bananas, sliced

TOPPING:

- 2 tablespoons flour
- ½ cup sugar
- 1 cup reserved pineapple juice
- 1 egg, slightly beaten
- 1 cup heavy cream
- ¼ cup grated cheddar cheese
- 3 tablespoons grated Parmesan cheese

In a medium bowl, mix the gelatin with the boiling water, stirring until it is dissolved; let it cool 10 minutes.

Stir in the soda. Refrigerate the mixture until it starts to congeal—45 minutes to 1 hour.

Fold in the marshmallows, drained pineapple, and bananas.

Transfer the mixture into a 9 × 13 × 2-inch baking dish, and chill until firm.

Meanwhile, make the topping by cooking the flour, sugar, pineapple juice, and egg over low heat in a small saucepan, stirring until it is thick.

Remove the pan from the heat, and let it cool; refrigerate until well chilled.

In a medium bowl, with an electric mixer at high speed, whip the cream until it is stiff; fold it into the chilled topping mixture.

Spread the topping over the gelatin mixture, and sprinkle with the grated cheeses.

If not serving the salad right away, return it to the refrigerator.

Serve the salad, cut in squares, directly from the baking dish.

Serves 10 to 12.

Reminder: Almost all varieties of flavored gelatin come in 3- and 6-ounce packages. Always double-check your recipe to make sure you are using the right size package because it will make the difference between success and failure!

FROZEN FRUIT SALAD

A very versatile recipe that can be used as a salad, dessert, or snack. Prepare these miniature salads ahead of time, and defrost and use them as needed.

---

2 cups sour cream
¾ cup sugar
2 tablespoons lemon juice
1 envelope unflavored gelatin
1 can (15 ounces) crushed pineapple, well drained
⅓ cup chopped maraschino cherries
⅓ cup chopped walnuts
2 to 3 bananas, thinly sliced

In a medium bowl, combine the sour cream, sugar, and lemon juice.

Add the gelatin, and mix well.

Stir in the drained pineapple, cherries, walnuts, and banana slices. Be sure to mix all the ingredients together thoroughly.

Spoon this mixture into paper cupcake liners set in muffin tins; freeze, uncovered.

When the salads are frozen, remove them from the muffin tins and place them in a large plastic bag or freezer container. Cover tightly, and return to the freezer.

Remove the salads and use as desired, but allow them to defrost for about 20 minutes before serving.

These salads are nice when served over slices of pineapple on lettuce leaves.

Makes 18 to 24.

Chapter 5
BAKED GOODS

Cakes
Pies
Pastries, Cupcakes,
& Cookies
Quick Breads
Yeast Rolls

Cakes

THE ULTIMATE CHOCOLATE CAKE

Once you have tasted this cake, you'll understand why I indulge in superlatives!

---

4 bars (4 ounces each) German Sweet Cooking Chocolate
½ cup unsalted butter, softened
4 eggs, separated
4 teaspoons sugar
4 teaspoons flour

Preheat the oven to 425 degrees. Grease a 9 × 5 × 3-inch loaf pan, and line with waxed paper.

In the top part of a double boiler, melt the chocolate over hot—not boiling—water, stirring occasionally.

Remove from the heat, and beat in the butter; let cool.

In a medium bowl, with an electric mixer at high speed, beat the egg whites until stiff peaks form; set aside.

In a large bowl, with an electric mixer at high speed, beat the egg yolks until thick and lemon colored.

Gradually add the sugar, beating constantly; add the flour, beating just until blended.

Stir in the cooled chocolate mixture.

With a rubber scraper, gently fold in the beaten egg whites until thoroughly incorporated.

Turn the mixture into the prepared pan. Reduce the oven temperature to 350 degrees. Bake the cake for 25 minutes.

Let the cake cool completely in its pan on a wire rack. The cake will "collapse," so don't panic. Refrigerate the cake in its pan for several hours.

To serve, loosen the cake by running a spatula around the

edge of the pan. Invert the cake onto a serving platter, and carefully peel off the waxed paper. Cut into ½-inch slices.

Serves 12 to 16.

HUMMINGBIRD CAKE

CAKE:

- 3 cups flour
- 2 cups sugar
- 1½ teaspoons vanilla
- 1½ cups vegetable or corn oil
- 2 cups mashed bananas (about 3 large, ripe bananas)
- 3 eggs
- 1 teaspoon salt

1 teaspoon baking soda
1 teaspoon cinnamon
½ cup chopped walnuts
1 can (8 ounces) crushed pineapple, undrained

ICING:

1 package (8 ounces) cream cheese, softened
½ cup butter or margarine, softened
1 teaspoon vanilla
1 box (1 pound) confectioners' sugar, sifted

Preheat the oven to 300 degrees. Grease and dust with flour a 10-inch tube pan or "Bundt" pan.

In a large bowl, mix all the cake ingredients by hand with a wooden spoon just until the ingredients are well combined.

Pour the batter into the prepared pan, and bake 1½ hours. The cake will crack slightly on top.

Cool the cake in its pan on a wire rack for at least 1 hour before removing. Then invert the cake onto a large serving platter.

To prepare the icing: In a medium bowl, with an electric mixer at medium speed, cream the cream cheese, butter, and vanilla until light and fluffy.

Gradually add the sugar, beating until the icing is smooth.

Spread the icing over the top and sides of the cooled cake, and refrigerate until serving. The frosted cake can also be frozen.

Serves 12 to 15.

HINTS

Vegetable or corn oil can be used interchangeably in most cake recipes, but never substitute olive oil for these two varieties as it has a very distinctive flavor—great for salads, but not for baked goods! To a lesser extent, peanut oil can also give cakes an unpleasant flavor.

To cut a fresh cake cleanly, use a wet knife.

CHOCOLATE-CHIP CAKE

This cake begins with a mix, but it certainly doesn't taste as if it did.

---

1 package (18.5 ounces) yellow cake mix
1 package (3½ ounces) instant vanilla pudding mix
½ cup vegetable oil
4 eggs
1 cup sour cream
½ cup chopped walnuts
1 cup (6 ounces) semisweet chocolate chips

Preheat the oven to 350 degrees. Grease and dust with flour a 10-inch tube pan or "Bundt" pan.

In a large bowl, with an electric mixer at medium speed, combine the cake mix, pudding mix, and oil, beating well to blend.

Add the eggs, one at a time, beating well after each addition.

Add the sour cream, nuts, and chocolate chips, blending well with a wooden spoon.

Pour the batter into the prepared pan, and bake for 1 to 1¼ hours.

Let the cake cool in its pan on a wire rack for 1 hour before removing.

Invert the cake onto a large serving platter, and store in the refrigerator until serving. The cake may also be frozen.

Serves 12 to 15.

HINT

All ingredients for cakes should be at room temperature before you begin.

PISTACHIO MARBLE CAKE

Here is another recipe that transforms an ordinary cake mix into a special dessert.

---

1 package (18.5 ounces) yellow cake mix
1 package (3½ ounces) instant pistachio pudding mix
¾ cup vegetable oil
1 cup sour cream
4 eggs
1 cup (6 ounces) semisweet chocolate chips
1 teaspoon cinnamon mixed with 1 tablespoon sugar

Preheat the oven to 350 degrees. Grease and dust with flour a 10-inch tube pan or "Bundt" pan.

In a large bowl, with an electric mixer at medium speed, combine the cake mix, pudding mix, oil, and sour cream, beating well.

Add the eggs, one at a time, beating well after each addition.

Pour one-half of the batter into the prepared pan.

Add the chocolate chips and the cinnamon-sugar mixture to the remaining half of the batter.

Add this half of the batter to the pan, and swirl through both of the batters with a knife.

Bake for 1 hour, or until cake tests done. Cool the cake in its pan on a wire rack for 1 hour before removing it.

To serve, invert the cake onto a large serving platter. If not serving right away, place the cake in the refrigerator until needed.

Serves 12 to 15.

HINT

Layer cakes are done if they spring back when lightly touched in the center. To test a pound cake for doneness, insert a toothpick in the center; it should come out clean.

CHEESECAKE

There are as many cheesecake recipes as there are cheesecake lovers, but this one is my all-time favorite.

CRUST:

16 graham crackers, finely crushed
6 tablespoons melted butter or margarine
½ cup sugar

FILLING:

4 eggs, separated
¾ cup sugar
  Juice of ½ lemon, *or* 2 tablespoons bottled lemon juice
1 teaspoon vanilla
2 packages (8 ounces each) cream cheese, softened

TOPPING:

1 cup sour cream
½ teaspoon vanilla
2 tablespoons sugar

To make the crust, combine the graham cracker crumbs, melted butter, and sugar, and press into the bottom of a 9-inch springform pan. (You can also use a 9 × 9 × 2-inch baking pan.) Set aside.

Preheat the oven to 375 degrees.

In a large bowl, with an electric mixer at medium speed, beat the egg yolks and sugar until well blended.

Add the lemon juice, vanilla, and cream cheese. Continue beating at medium speed until smooth—about 8 minutes.

Wash and dry the beaters well. In a deep bowl, with the electric mixer at high speed, beat the egg whites until stiff peaks form.

Using a rubber scraper, gently fold the beaten egg whites into the cheese mixture until thoroughly incorporated.

Spoon the filling into the prepared pan, and bake for 25 to 28 minutes, or until light brown on top.

Remove the cake from the oven, and let it cool on a wire rack for 15 minutes. Do not turn the oven off.

Meanwhile, prepare the topping by combining the sour cream, vanilla, and sugar.

After the cheesecake has cooled for 15 minutes, spread the topping over it, but not all the way to the edges.

Return the cake to the oven to bake for 5 additional minutes.

Let the cake cool on a wire rack for 1 hour. Then refrigerate several hours or overnight.

If using a springform pan, remove the sides of the pan before serving the cake. If using a square baking pan, cut the cake in squares to serve.

Serves 8.

Note: If you like fruit toppings, you can spread a can of cherry or blueberry pie filling over the cheesecake just before serving. This cake can easily be frozen, but not with the fruit topping, or it will get soggy.

HINT

Unless you know that your oven is fast, do not open the oven door to test a cake until the prescribed baking period has elapsed.

CHOCOLATE MARBLE CHEESECAKE

Two favorites—chocolate and cheesecake—combine to form a winning dessert.

CRUST:

1½ cups graham cracker crumbs
½ cup melted butter or margarine
¼ cup sugar

FILLING:

4 packages (8 ounces each) cream cheese, softened
2 teaspoons vanilla
1¾ cups sugar
2 cups light cream (or half and half)
2 squares (1 ounce each) unsweetened chocolate

Prepare the crust by combining the graham cracker crumbs with the melted butter and sugar. Press into the bottom and halfway up the sides of a 9-inch springform pan. Set aside.

Preheat the oven to 450 degrees.

In a large bowl, with an electric mixer at medium speed, beat the cream cheese and vanilla until fluffy.

Gradually add the sugar, mixing well.

Beat in the cream.

In the top part of a double boiler melt the chocolate over hot—not boiling—water; let it cool 10 minutes.

Transfer about 3 cups of the filling to another bowl, and mix it with the cooled chocolate.

Pour the plain filling into the prepared pan. Gradually, add the chocolate batter, barely stirring.

Bake the cake for 15 minutes. Then lower the oven heat to 300 degrees, and continue baking for 1 hour and 10 minutes.

Let the cake cool on a wire rack for 1 hour. Then refrigerate several hours until thoroughly chilled. The cake may also be frozen.

Just before serving, remove the sides of the springform pan.

Serves 16 to 20.

PUMPKIN CHEESECAKE

This recipe will please those who don't like the strong taste of pumpkin. It's great to serve at holiday time—or anytime.

CRUST:

   ¾ cup crushed vanilla wafers
   3 tablespoons melted butter or margarine
   1 teaspoon cinnamon
   2 tablespoons packed brown sugar

FILLING:

   4 packages (8 ounces each) cream cheese, softened
1½ cups sugar
   5 eggs
   ¼ cup flour
   2 teaspoons pumpkin pie spice
   1 can (16 ounces) pumpkin (do not use pumpkin pie mix)
   2 tablespoons light rum

To make the crust, combine the vanilla wafer crumbs with the melted butter, cinnamon, and brown sugar.

Lightly grease a 9-inch springform pan, and line the bottom with the crumb mixture. Set aside.

Preheat the oven to 325 degrees.

In a large bowl, with an electric mixer at medium speed, beat the cream cheese until fluffy.

Slowly beat in the sugar.

Add the eggs, one at a time, beating well after each addition.

Gradually beat in the flour, pumpkin pie spice, pumpkin, and rum.

Pour the batter into the prepared pan, and bake for 1½ to 1¾ hours, or until the filling is set.

Let the cake cool on a wire rack for 1 hour. Refrigerate several hours before serving. The cake may also be frozen.

Just before serving, remove the sides of the springform pan. Serve with whipped cream, if desired.

Serves 16 to 20.

HINTS

If your cake seems to be browning too quickly on top before it is thoroughly baked, place a pan of warm water on the rack above the cake in the oven.

There is a difference between regular (or all-purpose) flour and cake flour. If it is necessary to substitute all-purpose flour for cake flour, use seven-eighths of a cup for every cup of cake flour called for. Sift it twice, to make it lighter. Do not use self-rising or "instant" flour unless specifically indicated in a recipe.

DATE-NUT TORTE

   6 eggs, separated
1½ cups sugar
 12 ounces dates, coarsely chopped
1½ cups chopped walnuts
1½ tablespoons flour
   1 tablespoon baking powder
   2 cups heavy cream
   1 teaspoon vanilla
     Confectioners' sugar to taste

Preheat the oven to 350 degrees. Grease and dust with flour two 8- or 9-inch round cake pans. (Those with removable bottoms are easier to use.)

In a large bowl, with an electric mixer at medium speed, beat the egg yolks until thick and lemon-colored.

Add the sugar in three parts, beating well after each addition.

With a wooden spoon, stir in the dates and walnuts.

Sift the flour and baking powder together, and stir into the batter.

Wash and dry the beaters well, and in a deep bowl, with the electric mixer at high speed, beat the egg whites until stiff.

Using a rubber scraper, gently fold the beaten egg whites into the batter.

Spoon the batter into the prepared pans, and bake for 25 minutes.

Let the layers cool in their pans on a wire rack for 15 minutes.

Carefully remove the layers from the pans, and cool them thoroughly on a wire rack. (At this point the layers can be frozen or refrigerated for later use.)

About 1 hour before serving, in a large bowl, with the electic mixer at high speed, whip the cream with the vanilla and confectioners' sugar to taste until stiff peaks form.

Spread the whipped cream between the layers, and then frost the top and the sides of the torte with the remaining whipped cream.

Return the torte to the refrigerator until serving.

Serves 8 to 10.

HINTS

Cover dried fruit and nuts lightly with flour before adding them to cake batters. This will keep them from sinking to the bottom during baking.

To prevent a freshly baked cake from sticking to the plate, sift some confectioners' sugar onto the plate before placing the cake on it.

Pies

LEMON PIE

Tangy is the best word to describe this unusual pie.

---

2 lemons, very thinly sliced
2 cups sugar
2 sticks pie crust mix (or 1 box pie crust mix)
4 eggs

Place the sliced lemons in a shallow bowl; pour the sugar over them, and let the mixture stand for 2 hours at room temperature.

Meanwhile, make the pastry for a 2-crust pie according to the package directions.

Press half of the dough into a 9-inch pie pan; set aside the other half.

Preheat the oven to 425 degrees.

Beat the eggs well, and add to the lemon-sugar mixture.

Spoon this mixture into the prepared pie shell.

Cover the lemon mixture with the remaining dough to form a top crust.

Pinch the edges of the top and bottom crusts together to seal them.

With a sharp knife, make several slits in the top crust to allow steam to escape during baking.

Bake 15 minutes. Lower the oven temperature to 350 degrees, and bake another 35 to 40 minutes, or until the crust is golden-brown.

Cool the pie on a wire rack for 30 minutes. Chill thoroughly before serving.

Serves 6 to 8.

KEY LIME PIE

CRUST:

22 graham crackers, finely crushed
 6 tablespoons melted butter or margarine
 2 tablespoons sugar

FILLING:

 3 eggs, separated
 1 can (15 ounces) sweetened condensed milk
¾ cup lime juice (preferably freshly squeezed)
 6 tablespoons sugar
 1 tablespoon vanilla

Preheat the oven to 375 degrees.

To make the crust, combine the graham cracker crumbs with the melted butter and sugar; press into the bottom and up the sides of a 9-inch pie pan.

Bake for 7 minutes; let the pan cool on wire rack. Turn the oven heat up to 450 degrees.

In a large bowl, with an electric mixer at medium speed, beat the egg yolks until thick and lemon-colored—about 5 minutes.

Gradually add the condensed milk, continuing to beat.

Still beating at medium speed, add the lime juice, blending well.

Wash and dry the beaters very well, and in a deep bowl, with the electric mixer at high speed, beat the egg whites until soft peaks form.

Very slowly add the sugar, beating until the mixture is stiff and glossy. Beat in the vanilla.

Pour the lime mixture into the cooled pie shell. Top with the meringue, spreading to the edges of the crust.

Bake for 7 minutes.

Cool the pie on a wire rack for 1 hour; then refrigerate for several hours before serving.

Serves 6 to 8.

LIGHT AND LUSCIOUS ORANGE PIE

Convenience foods make this recipe easy enough for anyone to fix, but delicious enough for everyone to enjoy.

CRUST:

1¼ cups flour
  1 package (4 ounces) coconut cream pudding and pie filling mix
 ½ teaspoon salt
 ½ cup shortening
  2 tablespoons butter or margarine, softened
  1 egg

FILLING:

  2 cups sour cream
  1 can (15 ounces) sweetened condensed milk
 ½ cup orange-flavored instant breakfast drink (reserve ¼ teaspoon for garnish)
  2 cups whipped cream or prepared whipped topping

Preheat the oven to 350 degrees.

In a large bowl, with an electric mixer at low speed, combine the flour, pudding mix, salt, shortening, butter, and the egg. Blend just until the dry ingredients are moistened.

Press this mixture into the bottom and up the sides of a 9-inch pie pan.

Bake for 15 to 18 minutes, or until light golden-brown.

Cool the crust thoroughly on a wire rack before filling.

Prepare the filling by combining the sour cream, condensed milk, and breakfast-drink mix in a large bowl. With the electric mixer at high speed, beat until thoroughly combined—about 1 minute.

Spoon the filling into the cooled crust; refrigerate at least 1 hour before serving.

Just before serving, spread the whipped cream over the pie, and sprinkle with the reserved breakfast-drink mix.

Serves 6 to 8.

FUDGE BROWNIE PIE

---

2 squares (1 ounce each) unsweetened chocolate
½ cup butter or margarine
2 eggs
1 cup sugar
   Pinch of salt
¼ cup flour
1 teaspoon vanilla
½ cup chopped walnuts or pecans

Preheat the oven to 350 degrees. Grease a 9-inch glass pie pan.

In the top part of a double boiler, over hot water, melt the chocolate and the butter. Set aside to cool.

In a medium bowl, beat the eggs slightly.

Stir in the sugar, salt, flour, and vanilla, blending well.

Add the cooled chocolate mixture to the bowl, along with the nuts.

Spread the batter in the prepared pie pan, and bake for 25 to 30 minutes.

Let the pan cool on a wire rack for 15 minutes.

Cut the pie in wedges and serve warm topped with whipped cream or vanilla ice cream.

Serves 6 to 8.

REFRIGERATOR CHOCOLATE-CHEESE PIE

CRUST:

1 cup chocolate wafer crumbs
6 tablespoons melted butter

FILLING:

1 cup (6 ounces) semisweet chocolate chips
2 eggs, separated
¾ cup sugar
1 package (8 ounces) cream cheese, softened
Pinch of salt
1 teaspoon vanilla
1 cup heavy cream

This recipe must be made the day before serving.

Preheat the oven to 350 degrees.

Make the crust by combining the wafer crumbs and the butter; press the mixture evenly into bottom and up the sides of a 9-inch pie pan.

Bake the crust for 10 minutes; cool thoroughly on a wire rack.

Melt the chocolate chips in the top part of a double boiler over hot—not boiling—water; let it cool for 10 minutes.

In a medium bowl, with an electric mixer at high speed, beat the egg whites until soft peaks form. Gradually beat in ¼ cup of the sugar, and continue beating until the mixture is stiff and glossy. Set aside.

In a large bowl, with the electric mixer at medium speed, beat the cream cheese, the remaining sugar, salt, and vanilla until fluffy.

Beat in the egg yolks and the cooled chocolate.

With a rubber scraper, carefully fold the egg whites into the cheese mixture, blending thoroughly.

In a large bowl, with the electric mixer at high speed, whip the cream until stiff; gently fold into the chocolate-cheese mixture.

Spoon the filling into the cooled pie shell; refrigerate overnight before serving.

Serves 6 to 8.

HINT

Whereas egg whites should be at room temperature to whip successfully, whipping cream should be very well chilled. It even helps to chill the bowl and the beaters.

CRAZY CRUST PIE

A great recipe for those who love pies but who hate to make pie crusts!

---

   5 to 6 large apples (or 7 to 8 peaches), peeled, cored and
      sliced
3½ tablespoons sugar combined with 1½ teaspoons cinnamon
  ⅓ cup raisins (optional)
   4 tablespoons butter or margarine, softened
   1 cup sugar
   2 eggs
   1 teaspoon grated lemon peel
   1 cup flour

Preheat the oven to 350 degrees.

Place the apple (or peach) slices in a 9- or 10-inch pie pan. Sprinkle half of the sugar-cinnamon mixture over the apples. Sprinkle the optional raisins on top.

In a medium bowl, with an electric mixer at medium speed, cream the butter and the sugar.

Add the eggs one at a time, beating well after each addition.

Add the lemon peel and the flour, mixing only until ingredients are blended.

Spread the batter over the fruit, being careful to leave a 1-inch rim of fruit showing around the edge.

Sprinkle the remaining sugar-cinnamon mixture over the batter.

Bake the pie for 1 hour; let it cool on a wire rack for 1 hour.

Serve the pie at room temperature or chilled. The pie may also be frozen.

Serves 6 to 8.

CARROT PIE

This is very similar to pumpkin pie, but with a milder flavor.

1½ cups cooked and mashed carrots
 1 cup sugar
 1 cup milk
 2 eggs
    Pinch of salt
 1 teaspoon cinnamon
½ teaspoon nutmeg
½ teaspoon ground ginger
¼ teaspoon ground cloves
 1 9-inch unbaked pie shell

Preheat the oven to 350 degrees.

In a large bowl, with an electric mixer at medium speed, combine all the ingredients until well blended.

Strain the carrot mixture through a sieve, and spoon it into the unbaked pie shell.

Bake the pie for 1 hour, or until the filling is set.

Cool the pie on a wire rack for 30 minutes; then refrigerate for several hours before serving.

Serves 6 to 8.

HINT

To prevent the undercrust of a pie from becoming too soggy, you can either coat the surface with lightly beaten egg whites or softened butter, or dust it with a little flour. Another alternative is to partially bake the crust before filling it.

FRENCH MERINGUE PIE

It takes a lot of beating to create this pie, but it's truly unbeatable!

---

3 egg whites
⅛ teaspoon cream of tartar
1 cup sugar combined with 1 tablespoon unsweetened cocoa
12 Ritz crackers, finely crushed
½ cup chopped pecans or walnuts
1 teaspoon vanilla
1 cup heavy cream
2 tablespoons confectioners' sugar
1 teaspoon unsweetened cocoa or instant coffee powder

Preheat the oven to 325 degrees. Grease a 9-inch pie pan well.

In a deep bowl, with an electric mixer at low speed, beat the egg whites until frothy, and slowly add the cream of tartar.

At high speed, continue beating the egg whites until soft peaks form.

Gradually add the sugar-cocoa mixture, and continue beating until stiff peaks form.

Fold the crushed crackers, nuts, and vanilla into the egg whites.

Spoon the mixture into the prepared pie pan, following the contour of the pan.

Bake the meringue for 25 to 30 minutes, or until it is light brown.

Remove the pan from the oven, and cool thoroughly on a wire rack.

While the meringue is cooling, chill a medium bowl and wash the electric beaters.

Place the cream in the chilled bowl, along with the confectioners' sugar and the cocoa or coffee; whip until stiff.

Fill the cooled meringue with the whipped cream; refrigerate until serving.

Serves 6 to 8.

Pastries, Cupcakes, and Cookies

PECAN TASSIES

To make these miniature pecan pies, you will need tassy tins, which resemble small muffin tins. They are available at most well-stocked cookware outlets.

PASTRY:

    1 cup butter or margarine, softened
    2 packages (3 ounces each) cream cheese, softened
    2 cups flour

FILLING:

1½ cups packed light brown sugar
    2 tablespoons melted butter or margarine
    2 teaspoons vanilla
       Pinch of salt
    2 eggs
1½ cups chopped pecans

In a large bowl, with an electric mixer at medium speed, cream the butter and cream cheese until fluffy.

With a wooden spoon, stir in the flour to form a smooth dough.

Shape the dough into a ball, wrap in waxed paper, and refrigerate 1 hour.

Preheat the oven to 350 degrees.

Remove the pastry from the refrigerator, and divide into small balls, about 1 inch in diameter.

Press each ball into the bottom and up the sides of a tassy

tin. If you don't have enough tins, return the unused dough to the refrigerator until later.

In a small bowl, combine the sugar, melted butter, vanilla, and salt.

Beat the eggs, and add them to the sugar. Stir in the nuts.

Pour the filling into the unbaked pastry shells, filling each three-quarters of the way up.

Bake for 20 to 25 minutes.

Cool the tassies in their tins on a wire rack for 10 minutes.

Carefully remove, and refrigerate or freeze until serving.

Makes 2 to 3 dozen.

HINT

For pastries to obtain a well-baked, tender, brown under-crust, do not use a shiny pan. Use glass, enamel, or black steel.

MOCK CHEESECAKES

---

2 loaves (22 ounces each) soft white bread, with crusts
    removed
2 packages (8 ounces each) cream cheese, softened
2 to 3 tablespoons milk
1 cup melted butter
½ cup sugar mixed with 2 tablespoons cinnamon

With a rolling pin, flatten each slice of bread by rolling it
out once or twice.

In a small bowl, with an electric mixer at medium speed, beat
the cream cheese with enough milk to render it easily spread-
able.

Spread the cream cheese on each slice of bread.

Cut each slice of bread into 3 equal strips, and fold each
strip in thirds.

Dip each folded strip into the melted butter and then into
the sugar-cinnamon mixture. (The strips may be frozen at this
point and baked when needed.)

Place the strips on a lightly greased cookie sheet, and bake
at 350 degrees for 5 minutes.

Let the cakes cool on the cookie sheet on a wire rack for
15 minutes.

Serve them warm or at room temperature.

Makes about 8 dozen.

MOCK STRUDEL

While this recipe may not turn out like the strudel you buy in a Viennese bakery, it doesn't require the effort that real strudel takes either! Yet it tastes surprisingly good. It's lovely for Sunday-morning breakfasts at home.

PASTRY:

2 cups flour
2 teaspoons baking powder
2 tablespoons butter or margarine, softened
2 tablespoons vegetable shortening
   Pinch of salt
¾ cup milk

FILLING:

¼ cup melted butter or margarine
1 cup grape jam (approx.)—do not use grape jelly!
½ cup sugar mixed with 1 tablespoon cinnamon
1 cup raisins
1 cup chopped walnuts
1 cup shredded coconut

In a medium bowl, with a wooden spoon, mix together the flour, baking powder, butter, shortening, salt, and milk to form a smooth dough.

Divide the dough into two balls; wrap each in waxed paper, and refrigerate for 1 hour

Preheat the oven to 375 degrees.

On a lightly floured surface, roll out each part of the dough into a circle.

Brush each circle with the melted butter.

Spread the grape jam over the butter.

Sprinkle the sugar-cinnamon mixture over the jam.

Sprinkle the raisins, chopped walnuts, and coconut over the sugar-cinnamon mixture.

Starting at one side, roll the dough up tightly until it forms a long strip.

Place the strips on an ungreased cookie sheet, and, with a paring knife, make cuts ½-inch apart three-quarters of the way through the strips.

Bake the strudel for 20 minutes.

Cool the strudel on the cookie sheet on a wire rack for 15 minutes.

Following the cuts you made previously, cut the strudel into individual pieces, and serve warm. Strudel may also be wrapped in foil, frozen, and reheated.

Makes about 3 dozen.

BLACK BOTTOM CUPCAKES

These taste better than any cupcakes you have ever tried. Make a double recipe, if you like, and freeze half for later.

FILLING:

   1 package (8 ounces) cream cheese, softened
   1 egg, well beaten
 ⅓ cup sugar
    Pinch of salt
   1 cup (6 ounces) semisweet chocolate chips

CAKE:

1½ cups flour
  1 cup sugar
 ¼ cup unsweetened cocoa

1 teaspoon baking soda
  Pinch of salt
1 cup water
⅓ cup salad oil
1 tablespoon vinegar
1 teaspoon vanilla

Make the filling: In a medium bowl, with an electric mixer at medium speed, beat the cream cheese with the egg, sugar, and salt, until smooth.

Stir in the chocolate chips, and set aside.

Preheat the oven to 350 degrees. Place paper cupcake liners in 2- or 3-inch muffin tins.

In another bowl, sift together the flour, sugar, cocoa, baking soda, and salt.

Add the water, oil, vinegar, and vanilla, and mix well by hand.

Fill the cupcake liners about halfway full with the cake batter.

Drop about 1 teaspoon of the cream-cheese filling over the cake batter.

Bake the cupcakes for 20 minutes, or until the cake part tests done.

Cool cupcakes on a wire rack for 10 minutes before removing them from the tins.

Chill for several hours or overnight before serving, or else it will be difficult to peel the paper liners off of the cupcakes. They may also be frozen and served directly from the freezer.

Makes 2 to 3 dozen.

SO-SWEET BARS

1½ cups packed brown sugar
½ cup granulated sugar
½ cup butter or margarine, softened
3 eggs, separated
1 tablespoon water
1 teaspoon vanilla
2 cups sifted flour (sift before measuring)
1 teaspoon baking powder
1 teaspoon baking soda
¼ teaspoon salt
2 cups (12 ounces) semisweet chocolate chips
⅛ teaspoon cream of tartar

Preheat the oven to 350 degrees. Grease a 9 × 13 × 2-inch baking pan.

In a large bowl, with an electric mixer at medium speed, cream together ½ cup of the brown sugar, granulated sugar, butter, egg yolks, water, and vanilla; beat until fluffy—about 5 minutes.

Sift together onto a sheet of waxed paper the flour, baking powder, baking soda, and salt.

Slowly add the dry ingredients to the creamed mixture, mixing with the lowest speed of the electric mixer.

Press the dough into the prepared pan. Sprinkle the chocolate chips evenly over the dough, and then lightly press them into the dough.

Bake for 18 minutes.

While the dough is baking, wash and dry the beaters well. In a deep bowl, with electric mixer at high speed, beat the egg whites with the cream of tartar until soft peaks form.

Sift the remaining brown sugar, and gradually add it to the egg whites, beating well, until the egg-white mixture (meringue) is very stiff.

Spread the meringue over the dough after the 18 minutes have elapsed, and bake 10 minutes longer.

Cool the pan on a wire rack for 1 hour before cutting the cake into bars.

Serve the bars at room temperature, or freeze until needed.

Makes about 2 dozen bars.

COOKIE-BAKING HINTS

There are six basic kinds of cookies: drop, bar, molded, pressed, refrigerator, and rolled. For the molded, pressed, and refrigerated varieties, chill the dough before shaping it into cookies.

Work with only as much dough as you can handle at one time, leaving the rest in the refrigerator. By allowing the dough to stand in the refrigerator before use, you will have a less sticky dough because the moisture is thoroughly absorbed and the fat hardens. Molded, pressed, and refrigerator cookies contain a large amount of butter or margarine, and thus do not need to be baked on greased cookie sheets.

Drop cookies, on the other hand, are almost always baked on greased cookie sheets. Always use vegetable shortening to grease the sheets. If you use butter or margarine, the cookies will absorb the salt during baking and have an unpleasant taste. Drop cookies should be placed two inches apart on cookie sheets to allow for spreading while baking.

To keep crisp cookies crisp and soft cookies soft, place only one kind in a cookie jar.

SAND TARTS

½ cup butter, softened
½ teaspoon vanilla
1¼ cups sugar
1 egg + 1 egg yolk
2 cups sifted flour (sift before measuring)
1 teaspoon baking powder
½ teaspoon salt
¼ cup milk (approx.)
1 teaspoon cinnamon

In a medium bowl, with an electric mixer at medium speed, cream the butter and vanilla until light and fluffy.

Beat in 1 cup of the sugar, and continue beating until the mixture is smooth.

Beat in the egg and the egg yolk, mixing thoroughly.

Sift together the flour, baking powder, and salt onto a sheet of waxed paper, and add all at once to the creamed mixture, beating until thoroughly combined.

Chill the dough in its bowl, covered, for several hours or overnight.

Preheat the oven to 350 degrees.

Sprinkle a pastry board or a sheet of waxed paper with 1 tablespoon of the sugar.

Break off about one-quarter of the dough, and roll out as thinly as possible.

With a sharp knife, cut the dough into diamond shapes, and transfer to an ungreased cookie sheet. Repeat with remaining three-quarters of the dough.

Brush the tops of the diamonds with the milk. Combine the remaining 3 tablespoons of sugar with the cinnamon, and sprinkle over the diamonds.

Bake the cookies for 8 to 10 minutes, or until the edges are lightly browned. Remove to wire racks to cool.

Makes about 3 dozen.

RUGELUCH

This is a popular cookie recipe that is traditionally served during festive Jewish holidays.

DOUGH:

1 package (8 ounces) cream cheese, softened
1 cup butter or margarine, softened
½ cup sugar
2 eggs
3 cups sifted flour (sift before measuring)

FILLING:

¼ cup melted butter or margarine
½ cup chopped walnuts
¼ cup raisins
¼ cup sugar
¼ teaspoon vanilla
1 tablespoon cinnamon
1½ teaspoons grated lemon peel
Additional cinnamon for topping

Make the dough: In a large bowl, with an electric mixer at medium speed, beat the cream cheese and the butter until light and fluffy.

Slowly add the sugar, beating well.

Add the eggs, one at a time, beating well after each addition.

Gradually add the flour, beating only until the ingredients form a dough.

Divide the dough into 6 balls; wrap each ball in waxed paper, and refrigerate until firm—about 1 hour.

Meanwhile, make the filling: Combine the melted butter, walnuts, raisins, sugar, vanilla, 1 tablespoon of the cinnamon, and the grated lemon peel in a small bowl; set aside.

Preheat the oven to 350 degrees.

On a lightly floured surface, roll out one ball of the dough at a time into an 8-inch circle.

Sprinkle one-sixth of the filling over each circle, and roll up the dough into a long tubelike strip. Repeat with remaining dough.

Place all the strips on an ungreased cookie sheet, and sprinkle lightly with the additional cinnamon.

Bake the strips for 25 minutes.

Cool the strips on the cookie sheet on a wire rack for 30 minutes; cut into ½-inch slices. Serve at room temperature, or freeze until needed.

Makes about 4 dozen.

FORGOTTEN KISSES

This is a great way to use up leftover egg whites that accumulate whenever you make rich cream sauces or custards calling for egg yolks. Egg whites can be frozen until needed, but they should be defrosted to room temperature before you use them.

---

3 egg whites
⅛ teaspoon cream of tartar
¾ cup sugar
1 cup (6 ounces) semisweet chocolate chips

Preheat the oven to 375 degrees.

In a deep bowl, with an electric mixer at high speed, beat the egg whites and cream of tartar until soft peaks form.

Slowly add the sugar, beating well, until the egg whites are stiff and glossy.

With a rubber scraper, fold the chocolate chips into the egg whites.

Drop the mixture by teaspoonfuls onto a greased cookie sheet.

Place the cookie sheet in the oven, and immediately turn the oven off.

Leave the kisses in the oven overnight.

To remove the kisses from the cookie sheet, slide a metal spatula under each one.

Makes about 3 dozen.

Quick Breads

BANANA-YOGURT BREAD

A delicious (and nutritious) way to use up overripe bananas.

½ cup butter or margarine, softened
¼ cup sugar
1 egg
1 cup whole wheat flour
2 tablespoons wheat germ
2 tablespoons unprocessed bran (available at health-food stores)
1 teaspoon baking soda
½ teaspoon salt
1½ cups mashed bananas (about 3 medium, ripe bananas)
½ cup plain yogurt
½ cup chopped walnuts
½ cup raisins (optional)

Preheat the oven to 350 degrees. Grease and dust with flour a 9 × 5 × 3-inch loaf pan.

In a medium bowl, with an electric mixer at medium speed, cream the butter and sugar until fluffy; beat in the egg.

In another bowl, mix together the flour, wheat germ, bran, baking soda, and salt.

Combine the mashed bananas with the yogurt.

Add the flour mixture to the creamed mixture alternately with the banana-yogurt mixture; mix until well combined.

Stir in the nuts and optional raisins.

Spoon the batter into the prepared pan, and bake 40 to 45 minutes, or until the loaf is brown on top and a toothpick inserted in the center comes out clean.

Let the loaf cool in its pan on a wire rack for 15 minutes; then turn the loaf out onto the wire rack to cool completely.

Wrap the loaf in aluminum foil, and refrigerate for several hours for easier slicing. The loaf may also be frozen.

Serves 10 to 12.

HINT

When using sliced bananas in any recipe, you can prevent them from turning brown by marinating them for a few minutes in the juice of any canned fruit or in a little lemon juice.

ZUCCHINI BREAD

Here's a novel way to get kids to eat their vegetables (husbands, too). You can't really taste the zucchini, but it's what makes this bread so delightfully moist.

---

2 small zucchini
3 eggs
1 cup vegetable oil
2 cups sugar
2 teaspoons vanilla
3 cups flour
1 teaspoon salt
1 teaspoon baking soda
1 tablespoon cinnamon
¼ teaspoon baking powder

Preheat the oven to 350 degrees. Grease and dust with flour two 9 × 5 × 3-inch loaf pans.

Wash and dry the zucchini, but do not peel. Cut them into thick slices, and grate, a few slices at a time, in a blender or food processor. Set aside.

In a large bowl, with an electric mixer at medium speed, beat the eggs until light and frothy.

Add the oil, sugar, grated zucchini, and vanilla, beating well.

Sift the remaining ingredients together onto a sheet of waxed paper, and add to the bowl, mixing well.

Pour the batter into the prepared pans, and bake 1 hour.

Cool the loaves in their pans on a wire rack for 30 minutes; then turn the loaves out onto the wire rack to cool completely.

Wrap the loaves in aluminum foil and refrigerate for several hours for easier slicing. The loaves may also be frozen.

Makes 2 loaves; each one serves 10 to 12.

Yeast Rolls

With most of my dinner recipes, I like to serve French bread. Occasionally, however, I enjoy serving yeast rolls for an added touch. If your main course is fairly simple—or if you're serving a large buffet dinner—piping hot sweet rolls or brioches can enhance the meal immensely. Needless to say, they are also ideal for serving with any brunch menu.

If you've never baked with yeast before, you need not be afraid of failure. Just remember a few simple pointers.

Most failures with yeast recipes result from dissolving the yeast in liquid that is either too hot or too cold. In either case, it will kill the yeast. The liquid should be comfortably warm to the touch.

Any recipe using yeast must have a certain amount of sugar or honey to activate the yeast, so don't try scrimping on calories by eliminating it.

Most yeast recipes instruct you to let the dough stand in a warm place to rise. The top of your stove is the best place. If you have a pilot light, this will work very well. With an electric stove, place the dough on top of the oven and set the oven heat to 250 degrees to speed up the rising process.

The following three recipes are favorites of mine, not only because they're delicious but also because they require no kneading. Save these recipes for a lazy day when you feel like baking; freeze the results, and you'll have a ready supply of delicious rolls for any special occasion.

BRIOCHES

These buttery-rich rolls are delightful to serve with an elegant dinner or a Sunday brunch. You can also serve them alone with butter, jam, and coffee. Brioches keep beautifully in the freezer for several months. To reheat, simply wrap frozen brioches in foil and place in a hot (400-degree) oven for about 15 minutes.

---

    1 package dry yeast
   ½ cup warm water
   ¼ cup sugar
    2 teaspoons salt
    1 cup butter, softened
    6 eggs, at room temperature
4½ cups flour
    1 egg yolk mixed with 1 tablespoon water

One day before baking, sprinkle the yeast over the warm water in a large bowl; stir until the yeast is dissolved.

Add the sugar, salt, butter, eggs, and 3 cups of the flour. With an electric mixer at medium speed, beat 4 minutes, occasionally scraping the sides of the bowl with a rubber scraper.

Add the remaining flour, and beat at low speed for 2 minutes longer, or until mixture is smooth; dough will be soft.

Cover the bowl with foil (lightly oil the underside to prevent sticking). Let the dough rise in a warm place until doubled in bulk, about 1½ to 2 hours.

Using a rubber scraper, beat down the dough. Refrigerate, covered with foil, overnight.

The next day, grease 24 3-inch muffin cups or special 3-inch fluted brioche tins (available at any gourmet cookware outlet).

Remove the dough from the refrigerator; it will have a spongy consistency.

Turn the dough onto a lightly floured surface; divide in half. Return half to the bowl, and refrigerate until ready to use.

Working quickly, shape three-quarters of the dough on the board into a 12-inch roll. With a sharp knife, cut into 12 pieces. Shape each piece into a ball, and place in the prepared tins.

Using the same method, divide the remaining quarter of dough into 12 smaller pieces, and shape each into a small ball.

Dip your thumb in flour, and press an indentation into the center of each of the large balls. In each indentation, place a small ball of dough. Keep your thumb well floured for this operation to prevent sticking.

Cover with a towel, and let rise in warm place until the dough has doubled in bulk, about 1 hour.

Meanwhile, shape the other half of the dough in the same way, cover, and let rise as directed. (If using individual brioche tins, it will be easier to arrange them on cookie sheets.)

Preheat the oven to 400 degrees.

Beat the egg yolk with the water, and brush the tops of each brioche with the egg-yolk mixture.

Bake for 15 to 20 minutes, or until golden-brown.

Cool the brioches on a wire rack 5 minutes before removing them from the tins. Serve hot, or freeze in plastic bags until needed.

Makes 2 dozen.

CINNAMON ROLLS

DOUGH:

- 1 cup boiling water
- 1 cup shortening
- 2 teaspoons salt
- ½ cup + 1 teaspoon sugar
- ½ cup warm water
- 1 package dry yeast
- 2 eggs, lightly beaten
- 1 cup milk, lukewarm
- 6 to 7 cups flour

FILLING:

- 2 cups sugar
- 4 tablespoons cinnamon
- ½ cup margarine, melted
- 1 box (15 ounces) raisins

GLAZE:

- 2 tablespoons melted butter or margarine
- 1½ cups sifted confectioners' sugar
- 1 to 2 tablespoons milk

Make the dough: Place the boiling water in a large bowl, and in it melt the shortening; add the salt and one-half cup of the sugar. Cool slightly.

In the ½ cup of warm water, dissolve the yeast and 1 teaspoon of the sugar.

Add to the shortening mixture, stirring well, along with the eggs and milk.

Slowly stir in the flour, using enough to form a soft dough.

Cover with a towel, and let stand in a warm place until doubled in bulk, about 1½ to 2 hours.

Make the filling: Combine the sugar with the cinnamon.

On a lightly floured surface, roll out one-fourth of the dough at a time. Trim the edges to form a rectangle.

Spread the dough with one-fourth of the melted margarine; then sprinkle with one-fourth of the sugar-cinnamon mixture and of the raisins.

Starting at the long side of the rectangle, roll the dough up tightly. Cut into ½- to ¾-inch slices, and place on a buttered cookie sheet. Repeat, using the remaining dough and filling ingredients.

Cover with a towel, and let rise in a warm place about 2 hours.

Preheat the oven to 400 degrees.

Bake the rolls for 10 to 15 minutes, or until golden-brown.

Place the cookie sheets on wire racks to cool.

Make the glaze: Combine the butter with the confectioners' sugar; add enough milk to make a fairly liquid glaze.

Spoon lightly over the tops of warm rolls. Serve warm, or freeze until needed.

Makes about 6 dozen.

RUM BUNS

There are a few restaurants in Washington, D.C., that are noted for their rum buns. I wrote to one requesting the recipe, and the chef accommodated me by supplying a recipe that yielded 163 dozen! By intricate calculation, plus trial and error, I came up with the following recipe.

BUNS:
- 1 cup milk
- ¼ cup sugar
- ½ cup butter or margarine, softened
- 1 package dry yeast
- 1 egg, well beaten
- 2 teaspoons rum
- 1 teaspoon salt
- 3½ cups flour

½ cup packed brown sugar
½ cup raisins

GLAZE:

1½ cups confectioners' sugar
1 to 2 tablespoons milk
2 tablespoons rum
1 tablespoon melted butter or margarine

Carefully scald the milk, and pour it over the white sugar and ¼ cup of the butter in a large bowl. Stir well until the butter is melted.

Cool to lukewarm, and add the yeast, stirring until it is dissolved.

Add the egg, rum, and salt; mix well.

Slowly add the flour, beating well after each addition.

Place the dough in a greased bowl; cover with a piece of waxed paper or foil (lightly grease the underside to prevent sticking).

Place in a warm spot, and let the dough rise until doubled in bulk, about 1½ to 2 hours.

On a lightly floured surface, roll the dough out into a rectangle, about 6 × 9 inches.

Spread with the remaining margarine, and sprinkle with the brown sugar and raisins.

Starting at the long end of the rectangle, roll the dough up in jelly-roll fashion, and slice into ½-inch pieces.

Lay slices of dough on a buttered cookie sheet, cover with a towel, and let rise for about 1 hour.

Preheat the oven to 425 degrees.

Bake the buns for 12 to 15 minutes, or until golden-brown. Remove from the oven, and set the cookie sheet on a wire rack to cool.

Make the glaze: Combine the confectioners' sugar, milk, rum, and butter to form a fairly liquid glaze. Spread over the tops of buns while still warm.

Serve immediately, or freeze until needed.

Makes 18.

Chapter 6

DESSERTS

APPLE GINGER CREAM

---

3 pounds McIntosh apples, peeled, cored, and chopped
3 tablespoons butter
1 teaspoon grated lemon peel
3 tablespoons honey
1 tablespoon unflavored gelatin
2 tablespoons water
2 tablespoons rum
3 tablespoons chopped candied ginger
⅓ cup chopped walnuts or pecans
1 cup heavy cream
1 red Delicious apple
2 tablespoons lemon juice

Place the McIntosh apples in a heavy saucepan. Cover, and cook over low heat, stirring occasionally, until they are tender.

Add the butter, lemon peel, and honey, and continue to cook, stirring, until the mixture is very thick. Remove from the heat.

Soften the gelatin in the water for 5 minutes; add it to the hot apple mixture, stirring to dissolve the gelatin. Let the mixture cool to room temperature.

Stir in the rum, ginger, and nuts, and chill the mixture until it is quite thick.

In a medium bowl, with an electric mixer at high speed, whip the cream until it is stiff, and fold it into the cooled apple mixture.

Spoon the mixture into individual dessert dishes or into a serving bowl, and chill for at least 1 hour.

Just before serving, slice the Delicious apple, and dip the slices in the lemon juice to prevent them from browning. Use the slices to garnish the dessert.

Serves 6.

ALMOND GELATIN

The perfect finale to any Oriental meal.

---

  1 envelope unflavored gelatin
  ½ cup milk
  ¼ cup sugar
1¼ cups boiling water
  1 teaspoon almond extract

In a small bowl soften the gelatin in the milk.

Add the sugar and the boiling water, stirring until the gelatin and sugar are dissolved.

Add the almond extract; mix well.

Pour the mixture into an 8 × 8-inch pan, and chill for several hours until firm.

To serve, cut the gelatin into 1-inch cubes, and spoon into individual dessert dishes. Garnish with mandarin oranges, lichee nuts, or mixed fruits.

Serves 4 to 6.

PEARS IN WINE

When cold weather sets in, warm your guests with this dessert.

---

  5 firm pears
  4 tablespoons lemon juice
  2 cups dry red wine
  1 cup water
1½ cups superfine sugar
  5 whole cloves
  1 cinnamon stick
  1 2-inch strip lemon peel
 ½ cup red currant jelly

Peel and core the pears, and slice them in half.

Place the pears in cold water to cover; add 2 tablespoons of the lemon juice to that water, and set aside.

Combine the wine, water, sugar, cloves, cinnamon, and lemon peel in a stainless-steel or enamel-lined saucepan, and bring to a boil.

Drain the pears, and add them to the saucepan.

Reduce the heat, and simmer the pears until they begin to get soft. Remove them from the liquid, and set aside.

Reduce the wine mixture by one-third by boiling it rapidly.

Add the jelly to the wine, and remove the mixture from the heat

Stir in the remaining lemon juice. Remove the cloves and cinnamon, and discard.

Pour the sauce over the pears; serve hot or chilled, as desired.

Serves 6 to 8.

HINT

Before measuring syrup, jelly, molasses, honey, or other sticky substances, grease the measuring cup.

PRUNES FANTABULOUS

Prune lovers, rejoice! These are prunes at their finest.

---

1 box (16 ounces) large pitted prunes
1 cup Marsala wine
4 ounces cream cheese, softened
1 cup heavy cream

Two or more days before serving, place the prunes in a glass bowl or jar and add enough Marsala to cover them.

Let the prunes soak, refrigerated, for at least 2 days.

A few hours before serving, drain the prunes, reserving 2 tablespoons of the liquid.

In a small bowl, with an electric mixer at medium speed, whip the cream cheese with the reserved Marsala.

Pierce the prunes, and, using a pastry bag, stuff them with the cream cheese-Marsala mixture. Place enough filling in each prune to puff it up.

Arrange the prunes in a shallow serving dish.

In a medium bowl, with the electric mixer at high speed, whip the cream until stiff.

Place the whipped cream in a pastry bag, and, using a star-shaped tip, pipe the cream onto each prune, making a flower design.

If not serving right away, refrigerate the prunes.

Serves 4 to 6.

HEAVENLY FRUIT MELANGE

The ultimate dessert to serve at those extra-large, extra-special gatherings.

---

12 navel oranges
4 cans (16 ounces each) pitted black cherries, drained
2 cans (20 ounces each) sliced peaches, drained
4 cans (15 ounces each) pineapple chunks, drained
8 bananas, sliced
1½-2 cups Grand Marnier or other orange liqueur
½ gallon vanilla ice cream, slightly softened
1 pint orange sherbet, slightly softened
2 jars (12 ounces each) orange marmalade

Peel and section the oranges; remove the outer membrane from the sections, and chop them coarsely.

In a large punch bowl, mix together the oranges, black cherries, sliced peaches, pineapple, and bananas.

Cover the mixture with ¾ cup of the Grand Marnier.

Cover the bowl with foil, and let the mixture sit at room temperature for 1 to 2 hours.

One hour before serving, spread the vanilla ice cream and then the orange sherbet on top of the fruits.

Immediately heat the marmalade with the remaining Grand Marnier in a small saucepan.

Bring to a boil; reduce the heat, and simmer, stirring, for another minute or two.

Spread this mixture over the ice cream and sherbet; do not mix.

Refrigerate the dessert for 1 hour before serving. Toss and serve.

Serves 35 to 40.

EASY FROZEN AMBROSIA

---

  4 cups orange juice
½ cup lemon juice
2½ cups sifted confectioners' sugar
  1 cup heavy cream
  1 teaspoon vanilla

In a medium bowl, stir together the orange and lemon juices with 2¼ cups of the confectioners' sugar; mix until the sugar is thoroughly dissolved.

Pour the mixture into a 12½ × 8-inch glass pan or into 2 freezer trays, and freeze until firm—about 3 hours.

In a medium bowl, with an electric mixer at high speed, whip the cream until soft peaks form.

Gradually add the remaining sugar and the vanilla, and continue beating until the cream is stiff.

Spread the whipped cream over the frozen orange layer.

Return the mixture to the freezer, and chill at least 1 hour before serving.

Serves 6 to 8.

TRIFLE

A sensational dessert that serves a lot of people.

CUSTARD SAUCE:

  2 cups milk
  6 egg yolks
¼ cup sugar
    Pinch of salt
  1 teaspoon vanilla

TRIFLE:

¾ cup medium sherry
2 packages (10 ounces each) frozen raspberries, thawed and drained (reserve juice)
2 cans (16 ounces each) sliced peaches, drained (reserve juice)
1 can (17 ounces) fruit cocktail, drained (reserve juice)
1½ cups heavy cream
2 9-inch sponge cake layers, broken into 1-inch cubes
2 cups shredded coconut
1 cup slivered blanched almonds

Several hours before serving, make the custard sauce: Scald the milk in the top part of a double boiler over boiling water.

In a small bowl, beat the egg yolks, sugar, and salt.

Pour a little of the hot milk into the yolks, beating well; add the rest of the milk.

Return the mixture to the top of the double boiler, and cook over simmering water for about 10 minutes, stirring constantly.

Remove the top part of the double boiler, and place it over direct heat; cook, stirring constantly, until the mixture coats a wooden spoon.

Pour the mixture into a bowl, and stir in the vanilla. Cover and refrigerate until well chilled. The custard will not be very thick.

About 1 hour before serving, make the trifle: Mix the sherry with the reserved fruit juices.

In a large bowl, with an electric mixer at high speed, whip the cream until stiff.

To assemble the trifle, place one-third of the cake cubes on the bottom of a large attractive glass or crystal serving dish.

Sprinkle the cake with one-third of the sherry-juice mixture; the cake pieces should be fairly well saturated.

Combine all the fruits, and place one-third of them on top of the cake.

Top this with one-third of the custard, one-third of the whipped cream, and one-third each of the coconut and almonds.

Make two more layers, using the ingredients in the same order.

Refrigerate the trifle until serving. May be made several hours in advance if desired.

Serves 12 to 15.

VELVET HAMMER

Serve this as a dessert or as an after-dinner drink. The amount and kind of liqueurs can be varied to taste.

---

4 scoops (about 2 cups) vanilla ice cream, softened
¼ cup creme de cacao
¼ cup coffee liqueur

Just before serving, place the ice cream in a blender container.

Add the liqueurs, and blend well at high speed for a few seconds. The consistency should be thick, like a milk shake.

Serve the mixture in 5-ounce wine glasses.

Serves 4.

Note: *For a different flavor combination, blend the ice cream with ¼ cup each of Triple Sec and Cointreau.*

HINT

When a recipe calls for adding raw eggs or egg yolks to a hot mixture, always begin by adding a small amount of the hot mixture to the yolks first. This will moderate the temperature of the yolks so that when you combine them with the rest of the hot mixture, they will not curdle.

DIETER'S DESPAIR

Watch out for this one!

CAKE:

About 3 dozen chocolate sandwich cookies (Oreos or Hydrox
    are best)
½ cup melted butter or margarine
1½ quarts vanilla or chocolate ice cream, softened
4 egg whites
3 cups marshmallow creme

FUDGE SAUCE:

2¼ cups sifted confectioners' sugar
1 can (5 ounces) evaporated milk
½ cup butter or margarine
1 square (1 ounce) unsweetened chocolate
1 cup (6 ounces) semisweet chocolate chips
2 teaspoons vanilla

The day before serving, remove the cream fillings from the
cookies and discard.

Place the cookies in a blender container, and crumble them,
a few at a time, into fine crumbs.

Mix the crumbs with the melted butter, and press into the
bottom and up the sides of a 9-inch springform pan.

Pack the softened ice cream over the crust. Cover with foil,
and freeze overnight.

The next day, in a deep bowl with an electric mixer at high
speed, beat the egg whites until stiff enough to hold a peak.

Carefully fold in the marshmallow creme.

Spread this meringue topping over the ice cream in the
springform pan.

Immediately place the cake in a hot (450 to 500 degree)
oven, and bake for 3 minutes, or until the top is lightly browned.

Remove the pan from the oven, cover it with foil, and place in the freezer immediately.

Prepare the fudge sauce: Mix the sugar and milk together in a small bowl.

In the top part of a double boiler, over simmering water, melt the butter; add the unsweetened and semisweet chocolate and the sugar-milk mixture, and cook, stirring constantly, over gently simmering water.

When everything is melted and well blended, remove the pan from the heat and stir in the vanilla.

Pour the sauce into a container, cover, and store in the refrigerator until needed.

To serve, remove the sides from the springform pan. Serve the dessert, cut in slices, with the fudge sauce.

Serves 10 to 12.

BAKED ALASKA

If you thought this dessert was difficult to fix, read on.

CRUST:

1¼ cups vanilla wafer crumbs
¼ cup finely chopped walnuts
⅓ cup melted butter or margarine

PIE:

1 pint coffee ice cream, softened
1 pint chocolate ice cream, softened
5 egg whites
⅓ teaspoon cream of tartar
6 tablespoons sugar

Several hours or the day before serving, prepare the crust: Combine the wafer crumbs, walnuts, and melted butter, and press the mixture into a 9-inch pie pan.

Bake the crust at 350 degrees for 8 to 10 minutes; let it cool thoroughly on a wire rack.

When the crust is cool, spread the coffee and chocolate ice cream in the pie pan in two separate layers. Cover, and freeze until firm.

To make the meringue, place the egg whites and cream of tartar in a deep bowl; with an electric mixer at high speed, beat the egg whites until stiff peaks form.

Gradually beat in the sugar, beating until the mixture is stiff and glossy.

Pile the meringue on the frozen pie, and spread it to touch the edges of the crust. Return the pie to the freezer for several hours or overnight.

About 10 minutes before serving, remove the pie pan from the freezer, and place it on a cookie sheet.

Bake the pie at 450 degrees for 5 minutes, or until the tips of the meringue are just browning. Serve immediately.

Serves 6 to 8.

CHOCOLATE-NUT TRUFFLES

This confection makes a nice holiday gift. You can also serve these as a dessert with coffee and/or liqueurs.

1¾ cups semisweet chocolate chips
  2 tablespoons orange juice
  1 cup sifted confectioners' sugar
⅓ cup heavy cream
  1 teaspoon grated orange peel
  1 cup finely chopped walnuts, almonds, or pecans

At least one day before serving, combine the chocolate with the orange juice in the top part of a double boiler.

Heat the mixture over hot—not boiling—water until the chocolate is melted.

Using a rubber scraper, pour the chocolate into a medium bowl.

Add the sugar, cream, and orange peel. Stir until combined; then beat with a wooden spoon to mix it well.

Place plastic wrap or waxed paper directly over the surface of the chocolate. Refrigerate overnight.

The next day, sprinkle the nuts on a sheet of waxed paper.

Drop rounded teaspoonfuls of the chocolate mixture onto the nuts. With your hands, roll each spoonful into a 1-inch ball, covering it completely with the nuts.

Refrigerate the truffles, covered, until serving. They will keep well for several weeks in the refrigerator.

Makes about 2 dozen.

HINT

If you melt chocolate too quickly, it may start to harden up again. If this should happen, stir in a little melted butter or vegetable oil.

CHOCOLATE FUDGE ROLL

Don't serve this unless you are willing to share the recipe with your friends!

---

6 eggs, separated
¾ cup sugar
1 cup (6 ounces) semisweet chocolate chips
¼ cup water
¼ cup unswectened cocoa
1 pint heavy cream

Preheat the oven to 350 degrees.

In a large bowl, with an electric mixer at medium speed, beat the egg yolks and sugar until thick and lemon-colored—about 5 minutes.

In the top part of the double boiler, over hot water, melt the chocolate with the water; remove from the heat and let cool.

When chocolate has cooled, add it to the egg yolk mixture.

Thoroughly wash the beaters, and in a deep bowl, with an electric mixer at high speed, beat the egg whites until stiff; fold them into the chocolate mixture.

Grease an 11 × 17-inch jelly roll pan and line it with waxed paper; grease and lightly flour the waxed paper.

Spread the batter evenly around the pan and bake it for 20 minutes.

Remove the pan from the oven and cover the cake with a damp cloth for 15 minutes.

Place another damp cloth on a flat surface and cover it with a piece of waxed paper about 11 × 17 inches.

Sprinkle the cocoa evenly over the waxed paper.

Invert the cake onto the waxed paper covered with the cocoa. Carefully peel off the waxed paper that the cake was baked with.

In a large bowl, with an electric mixer at high speed, whip the cream just until soft peaks form.

Spread three-fourths of the whipped cream over the cake to within 1 inch of the outside edges.

Roll the cake up lengthwise, removing the waxed paper as you roll. Ice the cake with the remaining whipped cream.

If desired, garnish the top with a little grated chocolate.

Refrigerate the cake until serving.

Serves 10 to 12.

NO-BAKE CHOCOLATE PIE

1½ cups chocolate wafer crumbs
   6 tablespoons melted butter or margarine
  24 large marshmallows
  ¼ cup milk
1⅓ cups (8 ounces) semisweet chocolate chips
  ¼ cup strong brewed coffee
   2 tablespoons creme de cacao
   2 tablespoons coffee liqueur
   1 cup heavy cream

Several hours or the day before serving, combine the chocolate wafer crumbs with the melted butter, and press the mixture into an 8-inch pie pan.

In a heavy saucepan, over low heat, carefully melt the marshmallows with the milk, stirring constantly. Set aside to cool.

In the top part of a double boiler, over hot water—not boiling—melt the chocolate with the coffee.

Remove from the heat, and add the creme de cacao and the coffee liqueur; set aside to cool.

In a medium bowl, with an electric mixer at high speed, whip the cream until it holds stiff peaks.

Fold the marshmallow mixture into the chocolate mixture.

Fold the whipped cream into the chocolate-marshmallow mixture.

Spoon the mixture into the prepared pie shell, and freeze for several hours or overnight.

Before serving the pie, bring it to room temperature for 10 to 15 minutes.

Serves 8.

SNAPPY BREAD PUDDING

A wonderful cold-weather dessert that enables you to use up stale bread, while insuring that your family gets a nutritious dessert.

---

4 eggs
1 cup sugar
  Pinch of salt
½ teaspoon nutmeg
½ teaspoon cinnamon
1 tablespoon vanilla
1 tablespoon rum (optional)
4 cups milk, scalded
4 cups stale bread cubes
½ cup raisins

In a large bowl, beat the eggs until foamy.

Add the sugar, spices, vanilla, and optional rum, beating well.

Gradually stir in the scalded milk.

Add the bread cubes to the bowl, mixing until they are well saturated with the liquid.

Add the raisins.

Pour the mixture into a greased 2-quart casserole, and bake at 325 degrees for 1¼ to 1½ hours, or until a knife inserted in the center comes out clean.

Cool the pudding on a wire rack for 30 minutes before serving.

Serve warm, with whipped cream or vanilla ice cream, if desired.

Serves 8.

CANNOLI

An irresistible Italian dessert that can be made days ahead of time. You can buy cannoli forms at any gourmet cookware outlet. Or, improvise by rolling 6-inch pieces of cardboard into cylinders ½-inch in diameter. Staple them, and cover them completely with foil.

SHELLS:

1¾ cups flour
   Pinch of salt
2 tablespoons sugar
1 egg, slightly beaten
2 tablespoons firm butter, or margarine, cut into small pieces
¼ cup white wine
1 egg white, lightly beaten
   Oil for deep-frying

FILLING:

2 pounds ricotta cheese
¼ teaspoon grated orange peel
   Pinch of cinnamon
   Pinch of nutmeg
2 cups sifted confectioners' sugar
4 teaspoons vanilla
½ cup chopped candied citron
½ cup finely chopped semisweet chocolate chips

To make the shells, sift the flour, salt, and sugar into a medium bowl.

Make a well in the center of the flour, and place the egg and butter in it.

With your fingers, work these ingredients together.

Add the wine, a tablespoon at a time, mixing well after each addition.

When the dough begins to cling together, work it into a ball with your hands. Cover the dough with a towel, and let it stand for 20 minutes.

Roll the dough out on a floured surface to about $\frac{1}{16}$-inch thickness.

Cut the dough into $3\frac{1}{2}$-inch circles using a cookie cutter, and wrap each circle around a cannoli form; seal the edges with a little beaten egg white.

Fill a deep-fat fryer or skillet with about 2 inches of oil; heat to 350 degrees. Use a deep-fat thermometer if your utensil is not equipped with one.

Fry the dough until it is golden-brown.

Remove the shells with a pair of tongs, and drain them on paper towels. When the shells are cool enough to handle, remove the forms, and use them with the remainder of the dough to make more shells.

Cool the shells completely before filling. They can be made weeks ahead of time and stored in an airtight container.

To make the filling, place the cheese in a strainer, and shake out as much moisture as possible. Let the cheese stand in the strainer for 15 minutes.

Transfer the cheese to a medium bowl, and combine it with the remaining ingredients, mixing well.

Cover the filling, and chill it for several hours or overnight.

With a pastry bag, fill the cannoli shells with the filling, putting a generous amount in each shell.

If desired, you can dip the ends of the filled shells in chopped pistachio nuts and sprinkle sifted confectioners' sugar over them.

Keep the cannoli refrigerated until serving.

Makes 18 to 24.

BAKED CHOCOLATE SOUFFLÉ

Actually, there is nothing tricky about making soufflés if you use the right kind of dish (a straight-sided soufflé dish, usually made of porcelain) and if your egg whites are properly whipped.

The timing is somewhat tricky, however, and unfortunately baked soufflés cannot be made in advance. If you would like to serve this soufflé to company, it's best to assemble it just after you serve dinner. (You can have everything done in advance except whipping the egg whites.) Let the soufflé bake while you serve your guests coffee; that way, they can work up an appetite for your masterpiece!

---

2 squares (1 ounce each) unsweetened chocolate
2 tablespoons strong brewed coffee
½ cup sugar
2 tablespoons butter
2 tablespoons flour
¾ cup milk
   Pinch of salt
1 teaspoon vanilla (or rum or cognac)
3 egg yolks
5 egg whites
⅛ teaspoon cream of tartar

Generously butter a 2-quart soufflé dish, and sprinkle it with enough sugar to adhere to the bottom and sides.

Make a paper collar for the dish by using about 2 feet of waxed paper or foil; fold it into thirds; butter and sprinkle with sugar that part of the collar that will rise above the top of the soufflé dish. Attach the collar to the dish with cellophane tape or string.

In the top part of a double boiler, over simmering water, melt the chocolate with the coffee and ⅓ cup of the sugar. Remove from the heat, and let it cool.

In a medium saucepan, melt the butter, and stir in the flour with a wire whisk.

Meanwhile, bring the milk to a boil in a small saucepan, and add it at once to the *roux*, stirring vigorously with a wire whisk.

Add the salt, and cook over low heat until the mixture is slightly thickened.

Stir the melted chocolate mixture into the sauce, and add the vanilla.

Transfer the mixture to a large bowl, and let it cool 15 minutes.

Beat in the egg yolks one at a time, mixing well after each addition. The dessert may be made in advance up to this point.

Preheat the oven to 375 degrees.

In a deep bowl, with an electric mixer at low speed, beat the egg whites for 30 seconds.

Add the cream of tartar, and continue beating at high speed until soft peaks form.

Sprinkle the remaining sugar into the whites, and beat until stiff peaks form.

With a rubber scraper, stir a little of the egg whites into the chocolate mixture; then fold the remaining egg whites into the mixture, blending thoroughly.

Turn the mixture into the prepared soufflé dish, and bake for 35 to 40 minutes, or until the soufflé is puffed and brown.

Serve at once with sweetened whipped cream, if desired.

Serves 6.

HINT

If serving a large number of people, make two separate soufflés rather than trying to make a double recipe in a larger dish—it won't work!

Whipped Desserts

Nothing ends a summer dinner quite so pleasantly as a light, frothy whipped dessert. These refreshing concoctions are delightful any time of year, but they are especially welcome in warm weather.

Many cooks and cookbooks use the terms Bavarian, soufflé, and mousse interchangeably to connote whipped desserts, but there are distinctions between the three.

A classical Bavarian Cream always starts with a custard sauce (*crème anglaise*), which can be flavored in many different ways. This mixture is thickened with plain gelatin as well as whipped cream. It is placed in a dessert mold to set and is unmolded just before serving.

A cold soufflé is somewhat similar, except whipped egg whites are also folded in to give greater volume. Cold soufflés should be served in a straight-sided soufflé dish. If the dish is small (less than 2½-quart capacity), a paper collar may be necessary to support the excess mixture as it sets. This collar is made by folding a length of waxed paper or foil in thirds. It is then taped around the outer top of the dish, extending two inches above the edge. The collar is removed before serving.

A mousse (which means "froth" in French) is a sort of catch-all word for whipped desserts but, typically, it does not contain gelatin. It relies on either whipped cream or whipped egg whites—sometimes both—for its airy consistency.

Modern usage has obscured the differences between these three kinds of whipped desserts; and such ingredients as presweetened, preflavored gelatin have been introduced to simplify the cooking technique. But, however you prepare these desserts and whatever you call them, they will fit into almost any warm-weather menu.

MOCK STRAWBERRY BAVARIAN

This dessert is best when made with fresh strawberries.

---

1 **package (3 ounces) strawberry gelatin**
1 **cup boiling water**
1 **quart strawberries, washed and hulled**
2 **cups heavy cream**

Several hours or the day before serving, dissolve the gelatin in the boiling water in a medium bowl; refrigerate until it is partially set—about 45 minutes.

Set aside 1 cup of the most attractive strawberries for garnish; refrigerate them.

Crush the remaining berries with a potato masher.

With an electric mixer at medium speed, whip the partially set gelatin until it is foamy.

Fold in the crushed berries.

In a large bowl, with the electric mixer at high speed, whip the cream until it is stiff; fold it into the gelatin mixture.

Rinse a 2-quart dessert mold in cold water and spoon the gelatin mixture into the mold. Refrigerate, covered, several hours or overnight.

Just before serving, unmold the dessert onto a large serving platter and garnish with the whole berries.

Serves 8.

LIME DELIGHT

2 cans (6 ounces each) frozen concentrated limeade
1 package (6 ounces) lime gelatin
2½ cups boiling water
2 packages (3 ounces each) cream cheese, softened
4 egg whites
  Pinch of salt
  Fresh or frozen blueberries, sliced peaches, and raspberries
    for garnish

Open the cans of limeade, and let them warm up to room temperature.

Dissolve the gelatin in the boiling water, stirring to mix well.

Add the softened cream cheese, and with an electric mixer at medium speed, beat until the gelatin and cream cheese are thoroughly combined.

Blend in the partially defrosted limeade; refrigerate the mixture until it starts to jell—about 45 minutes.

With the electric mixer at medium speed, beat the lime mixture again until it is very foamy.

Thoroughly wash and dry the beaters, and in a deep bowl, beat the egg whites and salt until soft peaks form.

Fold the beaten egg whites into the lime mixture, and turn it into a lightly oiled 6-cup mold; chill until firm.

To serve, unmold the dessert onto a large serving platter, and garnish with the fresh or frozen fruits. (If using frozen fruits, they should be defrosted at room temperature for 2 hours, or to the icy-firm stage.)

Serves 6 to 8.

MAPLE-WALNUT BAVARIAN CREAM

Here is a basic recipe. Once you have mastered the technique, you can start experimenting with different flavoring ingredients in place of the maple syrup and walnuts.

---

 1 envelope unflavored gelatin
¼ cup cold water
¼ cup maple syrup (or maple-flavored syrup)
 1 cup milk, scalded
¼ cup sugar
¼ teaspoon salt
 3 egg yolks, well beaten
 1 teaspoon rum or vanilla
 1 cup heavy cream
 2 tablespoons very finely chopped walnuts
 8 walnut halves for garnish

The day before serving, soften the gelatin in the cold water, and set aside.

Place the syrup, hot milk, sugar, and salt in the top part of a double boiler.

Cook over hot, not boiling, water until the sugar is dissolved.

Add a little of the hot mixture to the egg yolks, and then return the egg mixture to the top of the double boiler.

Cook, stirring constantly, until the mixture coats the back of a wooden spoon.

Remove from the heat, stir in the softened gelatin, and let the mixture cool to room temperature.

Add the rum or vanilla.

In a deep bowl, with an electric mixer at high speed, beat the cream until it is stiff; fold it into the custard, along with the chopped walnuts.

Rinse a 6-cup mold in cold water, and spoon the mixture into the mold; refrigerate overnight.

Just before serving, unmold the Bavarian onto a large serving platter, and garnish the top with the walnut halves.

Serves 8.

WHIPPING CREAM HINTS

Do not be nonchalant about whipping cream, or it can turn into butter—very tasty, but totally unusable in dessert recipes! As soon as it starts to thicken, watch it carefully, and stop beating it as soon as it holds its shape.

It is best to whip cream in a deep bowl to avoid spattering.

To avoid confusion, my recipes tell you how much heavy cream to start out with. But, if a recipe calls for 2 cups of *whipped* cream, you should start with 1 cup of heavy cream. In other words, the amount of whipping cream is one-half the amount of whipped cream indicated. Always check recipes carefully for this distinction.

COLD CHOCOLATE SOUFFLÉ

---

2 envelopes unflavored gelatin
½ cup orange juice
1 cup (6 ounces) semisweet chocolate chips
¼ cup strong brewed coffee
¼ cup coffee liqueur
7 eggs (4 whole, 3 separated)
1 cup sifted confectioners' sugar
1 teaspoon rum or vanilla
1 cup heavy cream

The day before serving, sprinkle the gelatin over the orange juice to soften it.

In a heavy saucepan, over low heat, melt the chocolate with the coffee and the coffee liqueur.

Remove from the heat, and add the softened gelatin, mixing until it is thoroughly dissolved; set aside.

In a large bowl, with an electric mixer at medium speed, beat the 4 eggs and the 3 egg yolks until light and fluffy—about 8 minutes.

Add the sugar and the rum or vanilla, and continue beating for 3 minutes.

Add the cooled chocolate mixture, and beat until well blended.

In a medium bowl, with an electric mixer at high speed, whip the cream until it is stiff.

Thoroughly wash and dry the beaters, and in another deep bowl, whip the 3 egg whites until they are stiff.

Fold the egg whites into the chocolate mixture, and then gently fold in the whipped cream, blending thoroughly.

Turn the mixture into a 2½-quart soufflé dish, and refrigerate overnight.

Serves 8 to 10.

ORANGE-LEMON SOUFFLÉ

*This is a refreshing and tangy cold soufflé that can even be
served after a rich dinner.*

---

2 tablespoons unflavored gelatin
1 cup orange juice
¼ cup lemon juice
6 eggs, separated
   Grated peel of 1 orange
   Grated peel of 1 lemon
2 cups sugar
1 cup heavy cream

The day before serving, soften the gelatin in ½ cup of the
orange juice.

In a medium saucepan, over low heat, combine the remaining orange juice, lemon juice, egg yolks, orange and lemon
peel, and 1¼ cups of the sugar.

Cook, stirring constantly, until the mixture coats a wooden
spoon. (Be careful not to let the egg yolks curdle.)

Remove the saucepan from the heat, and add the gelatin-
orange juice mixture, stirring until dissolved. Refrigerate the
mixture until it is partially jelled—about 1 hour.

In a large bowl, with an electric mixer at high speed, beat
the egg whites until soft peaks form.

Gradually add the remaining sugar, beating until the mixture is stiff and glossy.

Gently fold the cooled orange mixture into the egg whites.

In a medium bowl, with the electric mixer at high speed,
whip the cream until it is stiff, and fold it into the soufflé.

Transfer the mixture to a 2½-quart soufflé dish, and refrigerate overnight.

Serves 8 to 10.

BEST MOUSSE EVER

Not only is this quick, but the taste is fantastic. Friends will be begging you for the recipe; and nobody will believe it was made in the blender.

---

  1 cup (6 ounces) semisweet chocolate chips
  1 tablespoon orange juice
  2 egg yolks
  2 whole eggs
  1 teaspoon vanilla
¼ cup sugar
  1 cup heavy cream
  3 tablespoons Grand Marnier
  2 tablespoons orange flavored brandy

In a heavy saucepan, over low heat, carefully melt the chocolate with the orange juice; remove from the heat, and set aside.

Place the egg yolks and the whole eggs in a blender container with the vanilla and sugar. Blend for about 2 minutes at medium-high speed.

Add the cream, and blend for another 30 seconds.

Add the cooled chocolate mixture and the liqueurs; blend until smooth.

Pour the mixture into six individual ramekins or dessert dishes.

Refrigerate for at least 8 hours, or overnight, before serving.

Serves 6.

HINT

To test an egg for freshness, place it in a glass of water. If the egg falls to the bottom of the glass and lies on its side, it is fresh. If the large end rises slightly, it is somewhat stale. If the egg stands on end and floats, it is very stale. The shell of a stale egg is usually shiny. If the contents of the egg rattle when it is shaken, it is not fresh.

Index

L

Lamb
    Couscous Tagine, 81–82
    Curried, 79–80
    Marinated, 78–79
    with Oyster Sauce, 70
Lasagne, 67
Lazy Cook's Bouillabaisse, 114–115
Lemon Pie, 195
Lemon Soup, 54
Light and Luscious Orange Pie, 198–199
Lime Delight, 251
Lime Pie, Key, 196–197
Liver
    Country Pâté en Casserole, 11–12
    Rumaki, 15–16
    Satay, 14–15
Lobster tails, Deviled, 113–114

M

Manicotti, 129–130
Maple-Walnut Bavarian Cream, 252–253
Marinated
    Leg of Lamb, 78–79.
    Mushrooms, 40
    Steak Kabobs, 62–63
Meatballs
    Sauerkraut balls, 13
    Zesty, 17
Mexican Shrimp, 109
Mock Cheesecake, 208
Mock Strawberry Bavarian, 250
Mousse, 249
    Chocolate, 256
    Crab, 22–23
    Salmon, 24
    Shrimp, 21
Mushrooms, 37
    Croustades, 38–39
    Florentine, 146
    Italian Stuffed, 36–37
    Marinated, 40
    Quiche, 126–127
    Soufflé, 128

N

No-Bake Chocolate Pie, 242–243
Noodle Casserole, Creamy, 141

O

Old-Fashioned Corn Pudding, 145
Onion Rounds, 29–30
Onion Soup, Best, 51–52
Orange-Lemon Soufflé, 255
Orange Pie, Light and Luscious, 198–199
Oyster Green Beans, 149

P

Paella, 104–105
Pasta, 118–119
Pâté, Country, en Casserole, 11–12
Pears in Wine, 231
Pecan Tassies, 206–207
Pie crust, 127
Pies
    Carrot, 203
    Crazy Crust, 202
    French Meringue, 204–205
    Fudge Brownie, 199
    Key Lime, 196–197
    Lemon, 195
    Light and Luscious Orange, 198–199
    No-Bake Chocolate, 242–243
    Refrigerator Chocolate-Cheese, 200–201
Piquant Chicken Breasts, 98
Pistachio Marble Cake, 187
Polynesian Chicken, 100
Poor Man's Lasagne, 67
Poppy-seed Salad Dressing, 171
Pork and Prunes à la Loire, 75–76
Potatoes
    Hawaiian Sweet, 154
    Salad Deluxe, 169
    Sinful, 156
    Tarragon, 155
Poultry, *see* Chicken
Prunes Fantabulous, 232

T

W

U

Y

V

Z